Delivered

Delivered

EXPERIENCING GOD'S POWER IN YOUR PAIN

BETH MOORE

W Publishing Group

An Imprint of Thomas Nelson

Published in Nashville, Tennessee, by W Publishing, an imprint of Thomas Nelson.

Published in association with Yates & Yates, LLP, www.yates2.com.

Abridgement by Kris Bearss.

Unless otherwise noted, Scripture quotations are taken from the Holy Bible, New International Version®, NIV®. Copyright © 1973, 1978, 1984, 2011 by Biblica, Inc.® Used by permission of Zondervan. All rights reserved worldwide. www.Zondervan.com. The "NIV" and "New International Version" are trademarks registered in the United States Patent and Trademark Office by Biblica, Inc.®

Scripture quotations marked AMP are from the Amplified® Bible. Copyright © 1954, 1958, 1962, 1964, 1965, 1987 by The Lockman Foundation. Used by permission. (www.Lockman.org)

Scripture quotations marked ASV are from the Authorized Standard Version. Public domain.

Scripture quotations marked ESV are from the ESV® Bible (The Holy Bible, English Standard Version®). Copyright © 2001 by Crossway, a publishing ministry of Good News Publishers. Used by permission. All rights reserved.

Scripture quotations marked HCSB are from the Holman Christian Standard Bible®. Copyright © 1999, 2000, 2002, 2003, 2009 by Holman Bible Publishers. Used by permission. HCSB® is a federally registered trademark of Holman Bible Publishers.

Scripture quotations marked KJV are from the King James Version. Public domain.

Scripture quotations marked NASB are from New American Standard Bible®. Copyright © 1960, 1962, 1963, 1968, 1971, 1972, 1973, 1975, 1977, 1995 by The Lockman Foundation. Used by permission. (www.Lockman.org)

Scripture quotations marked NKJV are from the New King James Version®. © 1982 by Thomas Nelson. Used by permission. All rights reserved.

Any Internet addresses, phone numbers, or company or product information printed in this book are offered as a resource and are not intended in any way to be or to imply an endorsement by Thomas Nelson, nor does Thomas Nelson vouch for the existence, content, or services of these sites, phone numbers, companies, or products beyond the life of this book.

ISBN 978-1-4041-0924-7 (hardcover)
ISBN 978-1-4041-0964-3 (ebook)

Printed in the United States of America

19 20 21 22 23 LSC 10 9 8 7 6 5 4 3 2 1

Contents

Introduction

A few days ago I stood in a line for something my Bible-study publisher called a "meet and greet." I had the joy of hugging at least a hundred and fifty studio-audience members for the Bible-study taping we'd just concluded. Laughter and happy testimonies filled the room and flooded my heart. By the time I hugged the last person, however, my mind was spinning from the more private things that had been whispered in my ear. One woman had recently lost a twenty-two-year-old daughter in a car accident. Another just behind her had buried a beloved three-year-old not long ago. Then I hugged the neck of a precious woman with a brightly colored scarf hiding the ravages of breast cancer that had recently metastasized to her brain. Beside her stood her sister, who was doing everything she could not to give way to bitterness. A few minutes later,

I embraced someone battling an eating disorder, then a pastor's wife whose husband had recently been invited out of their church. Another person slipped me a piece of paper and whispered, "Just read the note, but not right now!" The note was a request for prayer that she would be delivered from a long-term addiction.

Staring out the window on the plane ride home, I held open to God the letters I'd been given, as if He could see them better in hands at high altitude. I told Him again what I'll tell you: people are hurting. He already knew. I bet you did too.

Life can be excruciating. Crushing, in fact. The sheer magnitude of our worries can press down on our heads until we unknowingly descend into a pit of despair one inch at a time. Something so horrible can happen that we conclude we'll never be okay again. We can blow it so badly we think God would just as soon we stayed under that dirt and out of His sight. But, if we're willing to let truth speak louder than our feelings, and long enough that our feelings finally agree, we can be far more than okay. We can be delivered to a place where the air is crisp, the enemy is whipped, and the view is magnificent.

The words in the coming chapters fell completely fresh on me, as I pray with all my heart they will fall on you. They are not revisions of an old message. Each season of my life offers a new lesson, adds a new perspective, and the old fervor burns on and on. I suppose, as the chorus goes, "Redeeming love has been my theme and shall be till I die."

Yet it has never been enough for me to be free—I want you to be free too. It is not enough for me to know the thrill of God's presence—I want you to know it too. I want you to know the power of His Word that can defy every addiction, heal any affliction, and plug up every pit. I want you to know a love that is better than life. Because I have.

And I was a wreck.

I remember the first time I got an upgrade on a flight. I hadn't earned it with frequent-flyer miles. They'd run out of room in economy, and, since I was traveling alone, they told me they needed my seat and were moving me up. Throughout the flight, I was so excited that I acted like a five-year-old. I kept looking at the people to my right and left and saying, "Isn't this fun? Can you believe this? Can you believe we're sitting up here?"

Strangely, they could. I was a tad much for them. Not nearly cool enough. The whole time the flight attendant served us, I fought the overwhelming desire to hop up and help her. If I thanked her once, I thanked her a thousand times. The whole cabin was worn out by the time we reached our destination. I didn't get another upgrade for a while. I think the airlines sent out a memo.

Believe me when I say I got an upgrade from the pit, and I didn't earn it either. Though it's been years since I got it, I think about it every single day. A pauper to

God's scandalous grace, all I know to do with the over-flow is serve.

I'm writing to tell you I believe God has scheduled your flight out of a pit. Yep, you have an offer for an upgrade right here in front of you. You really can move up and out of that pit. If you'll grant me the privilege, I'd like to be your flight attendant for a while. I've taken this trip before. It's bumpy, but the destination is worth it. Thanks for having me along.

1

Life in the Pit

My man, our two dogs, and I just got home from a 1,700-mile road trip sewing five states together like a patchwork quilt. It's something we do several times a year.

When you insist on traveling cross-country with two sizable canines, you get to save your cash on motel rooms. We mostly stay in lodgings that have numbers in the names. I sleep between Keith (that's my man) and Beanie (one of the dogs), and from the sound of things, each has a deviated septum. I respond by turning up the air-conditioning unit, which in turn responds by freezing up and shutting down.

Folks who know how much we travel sometimes ask me why we don't get an RV. The answer, in a word: the bathroom. (Or is that two words?) The small space and lack of fresh air in an RV makes the presence of a bathroom so . . . well . . . inescapable. They say you get used to it, but do I really want to? Nope, the way I see it, we were not meant to get used to some things.

Like living in a pit.

But, unfortunately, we do. We can grow so accustomed to the surroundings of our pit that we wouldn't think of moving on without it.

Let's say for years you've been living in an old

RV so small, you can't stretch your legs or stand up straight. Visualize the clutter of too much baggage in too small a space. Imagine the unavoidable odor of that cramped lavatory. Your clothes even start to smell like it.

Now, imagine that you've been offered a brand-new home. A real one on a solid foundation with big closets and wide-open spaces. You can hardly wait to move in. Filled with anticipation, you rev up the motor of the old RV and plow it right into the new living room, taking out a wall or two on the way. Ah, finally! A new place to call home! You settle back in your RV seat, take a deep breath, and poise yourself to feel something fresh. Something different. Then it hits you: that deep breath tasted a lot like that old lavatory. You'd hoped for a change, but though you're somewhere new, everything feels and smells hauntingly familiar.

As disheartening as this realization may be, it could turn out to be the best news you've heard all year. If it wakes you up to the possibility that every situation you're in feels like a pit because you're taking your pit with you, you've just learned something you really need to know: you could quit driving that stinking RV around.

If you figure out you're the one driving that old RV, please understand right now that the last thing I want to do is shame you. The only reason I recognize a mobile pit-dweller is because it takes one to know one.

I just may have stumbled on the one thing I'm an expert on: life in the pit.

When it comes to pits, I guess I've lived in every conceivable kind. I've done the tour, trading in one model for another from childhood well into adulthood. A pit was my ever-present hell in times of trouble. And the only reason I have the audacity to write this book is because I'm not there anymore. I got out because something—*Someone*—worked for me. Trust me when I tell you this: if I can get out, anybody can.

Several months ago, God threw me into His Word to perform a sort of analysis of what a *pit* is exactly. I plopped open my trusty concordance, looked up every occasion where the term was used, and went to work. There, in the pages of Scripture, God showed me three ways we can get into a pit and a couple of ways we can get out. In the months that followed, I delivered some form of this message at three very different gatherings. The first was a group of four thousand women of all ages in California. The second was also a group of thousands, but comprised entirely of college girls. The third was a very polished studio audience at a taping for television.

Toward the end of each message, I asked the same questions. The first: "After all you've learned biblically about a pit, how many of you would say you've been in one?" In all three groups, every single hand in sight shot up into the air. The second question: "How many of you have gotten into various pits all three ways I spoke about?" Almost every single hand came up, mine included. I asked them to close their eyes for the last question: "How many of you would say you are in a pit right now? " To my surprise, a stunning majority of timid hands inched up—only shoulder high, just in case their neighbors were peeking.

So what's the big surprise? If I were a betting woman, I'd have wagered all three groups contained the cream of the crop of God-seeking, Jesus-following women. Many of them have been in Bible studies for years. Others look to them as the examples. As for the college girls, significant numbers of them sense God's call on their lives. Plenty are spiritual . . . and miserable.

I've come to the conclusion that vastly more people are miserable than not. Far more feel defeated than victorious. Yep, poker faces aside, they're in a pit. I've also come to the conclusion that some pits are just decorated to look prettier than others. Don't let anybody kid you, though. A pit is a pit.

That's the trouble. Too often we don't recognize a pit when we're in one. One reason some of you nicer folks are in a pit without realizing it is because, in our Christian subculture, we think a pit of sin is the only kind there is. But as we perform a biblical analysis of a pit, we're going to have to think much broader than that. So here goes: you can know you're in a pit when . . .

You feel stuck. Isaiah 42:22 says that a pit is a place where you feel trapped. You tend to feel your only options are to misbehave (i.e., have a kicking and screaming fit, hoping your flailing can help you escape) or submit (i.e., decide that you made your own bed and will die in it). Psalm 40 adds to the characteristics of a pit words like "slimy," "muddy," "miry."

Jeremiah 38:6 describes his pit as a place of sinking down. Imagine how much worse it was with sandals. No matter what's on your feet, you can take this fact to the spiritual bank: a pit only gets deeper. Low ground always sinks.

You can't stand up. In Psalm 69:2, David cried out, "I sink in deep mire, where there is no standing" (NKJV). If you're not already convinced, it's time you accepted the biblical fact that your soul has a very real enemy, and he is not flesh and blood. We can't keep on ignoring someone who is systematically trying to destroy our lives.

One way you can know you're in a pit is that you feel ineffective and utterly powerless against attack. You can't stand up to assaults, trials, or temptations because your feet are in the mud and mire.

I beg you to see that your enemy has a tremendous investment, not only in digging and camouflaging a pit in your pathway but also, should you tumble down, in convincing you to stay there after you fall in. He knows that in his pit you will feel powerless to stand up against him. There you are vulnerable to him and out of his way.

To the ancient Hebrews, a pit was a literal or figurative reference to the grave—to its threat—or to an abyss so deep the dweller within it felt like the living dead. Drawing from the figurative application, we'll define *pit* this way: a pit is an early grave that Satan digs for you in hopes he can bury you alive.

You've lost vision. Unlike that rank old RV, pits have no windows. Scripture paints them as places of darkness—the kind of darkness that impairs our vision. A pit is so poorly lit we can no longer see things that once may have been obvious to us. Without windows, we're convinced we have nowhere else to go. Yes, we can always look up—goodness knows that's the only opening we have—but we're often too focused on our sinking feet to crane our necks to the blinding sky. We become what the Bible calls stiff-necked.

Visibility extends no farther than six inches from our noses. We can't see out, so we turn our sights in. After a while, nearsightedness breeds hopelessness. We feel too buried in our present state to feel passionate about a promised future.

All image-bearers of God were intended to overflow with effervescent life, stirring and spilling with

God-given vision. We were meant to see ourselves as part of something so much bigger than we are. Something vital. Something incredibly thrilling. But the eyes of some of us have adjusted to the darkness of the pit surrounding us. We've forgotten what we used to see or shrugged off those early divine encounters as something we must have made up when we were less mature, just as Susan Pevensie did after returning from Narnia.

In the final Narnia story, *The Last Battle*, C. S. Lewis tells us that Susan, who in *The Lion, the Witch and the Wardrobe* witnessed the death and resurrection of the godlike lion Aslan, looked back on her times in Narnia as "funny games we used to play as children." She ultimately came to the conclusion that the heavenly land of her childhood experience was nothing more than a childish fantasy because she was "a jolly sight too keen on being grownup."

Dim vision ages us rapidly, and we lose the childlikeness that once made us feel like real princes and princesses in a kingdom. We can be young and yet feel old. Heavy laden. Burdened. In a pit where vision is lost and dreams are foolishness.

Through the pages to come, some of you will recognize your pits. For most of you, awareness won't come because you suddenly see how bad you are, but rather because you will wake up to how bored you are.

Getting out begins with waking up. *And* (this may be the hardest part) with being willing to feel again.

In Psalm 40:2, David exclaimed,

> He lifted me out of the slimy pit,
> out of the mud and mire;
> he set my feet on a rock
> and gave me a firm place to stand.

There you have it. We don't have to be in a stronghold of sin to be in a pit. We just have to feel stuck, feel we can't stand up to our enemy, and feel like we've lost our vision.

Ever been in a pit? Are you in one now? Is somebody you love in one? How in the world does a person get into these pits? More important, how does one get out? These are the questions we will answer in the rest of this book.

2

When You're Thrown into a Pit

*Y*ou can get thrown in. That's right, without doing one thing to deserve it and without wallowing your way into it. I'm not talking about a pit of sin here. This one's a pit of innocence. You can get thrown right into the miry deep before you know what hit you. Or worse yet, before you know *who* hit you. Those were the very circumstances surrounding the first pit mentioned in Scripture. Genesis 37:23–25 records the details:

> When Joseph came to his brothers, they stripped off his robe, the robe of many colors that he had on. Then they took him and threw him into the pit. The pit was empty; there was no water in it. Then they sat down to eat a meal. (HCSB)

In a fit of jealous rage set up by their father's partiality, the older sons of Jacob threw their seventeen-year-old little brother, Joseph, into a cistern with the intention of leaving him for dead. Let that sink in a second. Perhaps you've read the story so many times the brothers' actions no longer seem like a big deal. After all, things turned out okay, right?

I sat across the table from a gifted woman of God not long ago who told me that when she was little, her father put her out of the car on a country road because she was crying. He then proceeded to drive off. He came back and got her a little later, his feathers puffed up like a rooster, hoping she'd learned a lesson. She learned a lesson all right: she learned she couldn't trust her father.

In spite of all I've seen and heard, when she told me this story, it was all I could do to keep my chin off the floor. I was utterly horrified. Since this woman has been greatly used of God, you might reason that things turned out okay for her too. But I assure you, the price of her redemption was sky high. Every day she must consciously make the choice to believe her godly husband is not going to drop her off somewhere and never come back. Never minimize the choice someone like her makes daily to dig her heels securely in the rock and not slip back in that familiar pit that continually beckons, "Come home! Come home!"

The New King James Version words Psalm 40:2 this way: "[God] also brought me up out of a horrible pit." Yep, that says it. Some pits are just plain horrible. And when we sit across from someone bearing witness to one of these, horror can be an appropriate first response. I hope never to reach the point where I cease to cry over some of the stories I hear. Every story you hear, every account you read, happens to real, live, flesh and blood that bruises, gushes, and scars. So many of the people surrounding us have suffered horrifically in a pit they did not dig for themselves. Often, they first need the simple validation of someone saying to them, "That is *horrible*. I am so sorry that I hardly know what to say." Then, when trust is earned and the time is right, we can testify to our hope.

The ways we can get thrown into a pit are as varied as the footprints planted in them:

- Like my young friends, Cara, Christen, and Amanda, who watched a drunk teenager drive her car off the road, into the yard, and over their mother, you can be thrown into a pit by sudden tragedy.
- Like one precious woman in Bible study, who was stabbed repeatedly by a boyfriend she tried to break up with, you can be thrown into the pit by a violent crime.
- Like my family of origin, you can be thrown into a pit by a loved one suffering from mental illness.
- Also, like my family, you can be thrown into a pit by an alcoholic leaving a deep path of destruction too wide to avoid. (I cast no condemnation on this loved one. There but for the grace of God should I have gone.)
- Like my friend Sara, you can be thrown into a pit by your spouse's declaration that, after twenty years of marriage, he's in love with someone else, and he's leaving.
- Like Sara's children, you can be thrown into a pit by a parent who suddenly abandons the home.

- Like Eric, a brother in Christ, you can be thrown into a pit by a heartless woman who says you've bored her to tears and she's going to have some fun without you.
- Like my friend Shawn, and staggering numbers of others, you can be thrown into the pit by a life-threatening disease. Even imminent death.
- Like Jim and Connie, you can be thrown into a pit by the birth of a severely handicapped child who may never recognize your face but will probably outlive you.
- Like Charles and Gayle, you can be thrown into a pit by a house fire that happened in one brief window of opportunity when you had no insurance.
- Like numerous members of my church in Houston, you can be thrown into a pit by traumatic financial loss when a company like Enron comes tumbling down.
- Or, like so many children standing in the same line with Melissa and me as we waited to see a loved one who was doing time in jail, you can be thrown into a pit by a crackhead parent who rarely sobers up enough to care. Make no mistake. A pit offers ready residence to the rich and poor alike. Pain couldn't care less about your social status.
- Like me, you can be thrown into a pit by a close relative selfish and sick enough to molest you when you were a child.

- Like my husband, Keith, you can be thrown into the pit by the sudden death of a sibling while you were playing together and, like him, end up wishing it had been you.
- Also like my husband, you can be thrown into a pit when you lose yet another sibling and you're left to wonder why some families suffer so much more than others. Life is danged unfair.
- Give this one a little extra reverence with me: Like Mary, Sue, Ginny, Heather, Buddy, Randy, and so many others with real names and real pain, you can be thrown into a pit by the death of a beloved, irreplaceable child.
- Like you . . . ?

These examples are no more fun for me to write than they are for you to read. But I don't know how we're ever going to get out of a pit we refuse to recognize or talk about. Mind you, we could experience blows like these without necessarily descending into the pit, but the chances of enduring such horrors without entering the darkness for at least a little while are about as good as Joseph gripping the edges of that cistern and resisting the shove of his brothers. The downward force of some circumstances can be almost too much to resist.

Many of us found ourselves in a pit long before we reached Joseph's age. To be completely candid with you, I don't even remember life before the pit. I demonstrated behavioral patterns of a victim of abuse long before I went to kindergarten. The earlier we enter the pit or the longer we stay, the more it feels like home. We start hanging our pictures on the wall, tidying up the place, and making ourselves comfortable. If we're cool enough, we may even move a Pottery Barn couch and Williams-Sonoma kitchenware right into the middle of it. But as soon as the rain comes, it all gets soiled. That's the trouble. Every pit has a dirt floor.

Of all three ways to get into a pit, getting thrown in—not by *something* but by *someone*—can be the most complicated to deal with emotionally and spiritually. I'll give you a few reasons why.

For starters, when someone throws us in, we obviously have someone to blame. *It's all their fault.* Talk about a scenario with the capacity to eat us alive! Often when someone else puts us in a pit, we know in the depths of our heart that it wasn't his or her intention. Take, for instance, a family member with mental illness, or a parent who neglects her healthy children because she can't help focusing most of her attention on one desperately handicapped child. As much as pain can skew our thinking, motives and intentions still mean a great deal to us, and knowing that someone never meant to hurt us can lift us considerably in our ascent from the pit. The emotions involved are still complicated, but not nearly as much as they could be had the hurt been intentional.

You want to talk complications? Okay, how about times when you've been thrown into the pit by someone else's sin, and that someone happens to be a family member? Or a loved one who was supposed to love you back? Getting over the trauma would have been hard enough had Joseph been thrown into the pit by strangers who picked him randomly. Instead, his own flesh and blood did it . . . and they meant to. Look once again at the excerpt from Genesis that I quoted earlier. I purposely included that insidious last line that tells how Joseph's brothers, after throwing him into the pit, "then . . . sat down to eat a meal." Ponder that a moment. They'd just thrown their own kicking and screaming sibling into a deep hole, yet they apparently weren't sick to their stomachs. They didn't run for their lives. They sat right there, pulled out their PB&Js, and ate lunch. Infuriating, isn't it?

Genesis 42:21 describes what was emanating from the pit while the brothers had their picnic. The Amplified Bible says it best: "We saw the distress and anguish of his soul when he begged us [to let him go], and we would not hear."

What about times when a person has been used by the enemy to throw us into a pit, and he or she remains close by, lives on as if nothing has ever happened, sees our distress and anguish, but *will not hear* us? Maybe even despises us for our weakness. Ah, now that's complicated. What's even more tragic is the humiliating lengths we'll go to in order to make someone hear us, and all we end up doing is digging our pits deeper. How often have I made a fool of myself just trying to get someone who hurt me to hear me?

Beloved, I hate to bring up this word, but I just don't have a choice. It's the last word any of us want echoing back and forth in a pit we've been thrown into. But we must open our ears and hear that difficult word again: *forgive.* It's a tough thing to do, but we must forgive, even—no, *especially*—those who don't care to be forgiven.

Through the infused power of His own Spirit, forgive like Christ forgave when He said, "Father, forgive them, for they do not know what they are doing." Translation: "They don't have a clue." Whoever threw you into the pit doesn't have any idea how much it hurt you. How much it affected your decisions and relationships. I'm not sure they would get it even if you told them in detail. Humbly but very specifically, forgive them not only for their destructive actions but for their *ignorance.* You have no other choice if you want out of that pit.

I know you've heard all of this a thousand times, but this could be the day it sinks in, dear one. This could be the day of your deliverance. You think you can't do it? I felt the same way. I heard over and over how I'd have to forgive, but I just folded my arms over my chest in a huff and refused to do anything about it. You see,

I started out in a pit of innocence, but, through the years, my bitterness rearranged the furniture until it was nothing more than a well-camouflaged pit of sin. I thought forgiving my pit-throwers would make what happened all right. It didn't. Still hasn't. What I didn't understand about forgiveness was that it would make *me* all right. One day I finally began getting the message, and I'm praying right now that this is that day for you.

I want to tell you a few things that have helped me in my ascent out of the pit of unforgiveness. God changed the way I looked at the entire situation when I began to see that my grudge against people who hurt me only strengthened the grip of my bondage to them. The Greek word translated "nursed a grudge against" in Mark 6:19 means "to hold on, endure. . . . Metaphorically, to be held in or by anything; to be entangled in something, be enmeshed, to be subject to." How do you like that? Our grudges only work to further entangle and enmesh us with the persons we won't forgive. How ironic! When we won't forgive, the people we often want to be around least because they've hurt us so badly are the very people we take with us emotionally everywhere we go. Get this: we are "subject to" them through our own unforgiveness. Do you want to be subject to someone who has hurt you terribly? Neither do I.

I'll tell you something else that helped me greatly.

Somehow the thought of having to forgive only made me feel more abused, as if I was forced to be passive to the perpetrator once again. My breakthrough came when I realized that nothing took more divine power than forgiveness, and therefore, nothing was more powerful than forgiving.

You will never use your own volition—the force of your will—more dramatically than when you agree with God to start forgiving. Forgiveness is not about feeling. It's about *willing*. No stronger force exists. Forgiveness was the force that kept Christ, by His own submission, nailed to that cross. He could have taken Himself down in a split second. He could have called upon every archangel in the heavens, armed and ready. Forgiveness is not passivity, dear one. It is the ability to withstand the pressing, quaking gates of hell. Take this power and wield it. It's your right as a child of God. In the power of Jesus, first you will it and soon you'll feel it.

The Christian experience teems with so many paradoxes like this. It does take far more strength and personal fortitude to fall on our knees and submit to God than to stand and fight our endless battles for significance. Don't let anyone make you think that forgiveness is a covenant with weakness. Nothing demands more elbow grease than thrusting your arms forward and giving God the solitary right to vengeance.

There can be a couple of other scenarios that make blame equally irresistible. The book of Job suggests them both. It's not coincidental that Job refers to a pit numerous times, because nothing invites us to draw near to an early grave like suffering and loss. Simply put, suffering and loss can make us wish we were dead. And since Satan wishes the same thing, his job is to keep us in that morbid mind-set. In such anguish of soul, our human natures thrash and grasp about for someone to blame when things go wrong.

Job's friends tried to get him to blame himself. Or, if you're like me, it was more often at the insistence of your own secret self-loathing. Haven't most of us felt the sickening urge toward self-blame? *It's all my fault.* One reason Satan continues his self-employment as the accuser (Revelation 12:10) is because he knows that even when we're innocent of any reason for being in a pit, we are well aware that we are far from innocent in other things. He plays mind games with our consciences so that, for the life of us, we can't seem to distinguish between those areas where we are guilty and those where we are innocent.

For instance, a woman who has been raped may be tormented by memories of times when she wasn't innocent in physical relationships in the past. She now listens to the accuser, loses her ability to discriminate, and decides she must have asked to be raped. *Wrong.*

23

A man abandoned by his wife can decide he deserved to be left because he worked too hard. *Nope.* Maybe he deserved some serious confrontations. Maybe he deserved to be dragged into counseling. But did he deserve a divorce?

Their kids take on guilt because they are certain that what really caused the breakup was the fighting between themselves. They knew they should have quit. And they should have cleaned up their rooms. Now look what they've caused.

Behold the added havoc the enemy can wreak when he suggests ever so cleverly that you dug that pit, it fits you, and you'd better crawl in it.

Listen carefully: you can be in a pit innocently even if you haven't always been innocent. Give yourself a break. No one but the smallest child has *always* been innocent. So maybe the question is not, "Have you done *anything* wrong?" Maybe the better question is, "Have you done the wrong that fits the pit?" If you have, well, so have I, and we'll deal with that in the next few chapters. If you haven't, you're in a pit of innocence . . . whether or not you're unarguably innocent in every other area of your life.

Satan is a master at using our own insecurity against us. He knows that, deep in our hearts, we're so fragile and injured by life that his faintest whisper will talk us into feeling guilty even when we're not. We have some problems all right—we are broken and flawed—but problems by themselves don't dig pits. They just offer shovels. We provide the sweat.

We have one other place to go before we can finish this chapter: *It's all God's fault.* What do we do when we feel God is to blame for the pit we're in? Like when we've lost a loved one or lost our health? From all the free counsel Job was getting, he could either follow his friends' advice and blame himself, or he could follow his wife's advice (and perhaps his own gut) and blame God. The problem with blaming God is that it charges Him with wrongdoing. Thankfully, "He knows how we are formed, he remembers that we are dust" (Psalm 103:14). In other words, He understands us and He takes into account our limitations.

We, on the other hand, are totally incapable of understanding His ways at times. Yet in His tender mercy, God lets us ask the same nagging question that Abraham posed: "Will not the Judge of all the earth do right?" Maybe we ask it using different words, such as, "Can we really be sure that God always has our best interests at heart?" Or maybe we just say it silently, letting our distancing hearts speak for themselves. If we're willing to stay close enough and watch long enough, we will discover that the answer to the question is emphatically *yes*. The Judge of all the earth will do right. He is complete perfection. All wise. Only good.

Satan has no more effective weapon in his arsenal than to make us question whether God is really good. He knows God alone possesses the power and passion for us to be restored after nearly being shredded in life's killing fields. For Satan to talk us into distrusting God and distancing ourselves from Him is to keep us broken, ineffective, and, frankly, out of his hair.

I have a darling twelve-year-old friend at my church named Kendall. I have known Kendall all her life and prayed for her from the time the doctor first discovered her Down syndrome. She has mainstreamed in sports and in school. I was told the first time she ran a base in softball and the first time she finished every lap at her swim meet. She and I like to wear our black boots to church on the same days. I am crazy about her.

Characteristically active, talkative, and cheerful, Kendall became dramatically lethargic and increasingly pale a few months ago. We were all astounded when the medical tests proved positive for leukemia. No, not just astounded. Horrified. In the privacy of my own safe and sound relationship with God, the news sent me whirling. Didn't Kendall have enough to deal with? Didn't her family? Why her? Why not me? And if my emotions whirled at Kendall's bad news, can you imagine what her family felt? (Even now, I can hardly see to write for the tears in my eyes.)

Soon after Kendall was diagnosed, I had to have some medical tests of my own. She and I text-messaged one another from our different hospitals. She prayed for me; I prayed for her. The guilt threatened to overwhelm me when my tests came out clear after hers didn't. Maybe she'd just outprayed me.

In God's grace and patience, He let me whirl and land feet first upon Zephaniah 3:5: "The LORD within her is righteous. He does no wrong . . . every new day he does not fail." The verse describes Jerusalem, but I believe God used it in that moment to speak to me about Kendall, His precious child who openly, confidently calls His Son Savior.

The Lord is within her through His Holy Spirit. And He is righteous. And He does no wrong. As I sat before the God I love and trust, I drank those words like tonic—and I wept. My feelings were hurt. Not because God was wrong, but because my feelings are at times such poor reflections of truth. Right there in His presence, I recounted what I knew to be true, and, before long, it changed what I felt. No, I can't explain how the whole goodness-of-God, suffering-of-man thing works, but I know that God cannot—does not—wrong His children. He can't. Inconceivably holy, God cannot sin. He is unapproachable Light, and He has no dark side.

At the end of the book of Job, its protagonist didn't have his original questions answered either, but this he knew: his God was huge, his God was wise, and his God would redeem. Charging God with wrongdoing will only dig us into a deeper pit. However, holding God ultimately responsible in the healthy way, as His Word suggests, will be our ticket out.

Stick with me here. I know I've just made a statement that I need to unpack. How we react to our remaining discussion in this chapter will determine whether we stay in or get out of that pit we've been thrown into.

Think back on Joseph, our first scriptural example of a pit-dweller who did not dig his way into it. He had plenty of people he could blame. A grudge, however, would only have kept his feet buried in the bottom of his pit. Somewhere along the way, Joseph decided not only to look up but also to point up. His decision to view God as entirely sovereign and ultimately responsible was the life of him. Why? Because he knew God could only be good and do right. The words Joseph spoke over his guilty brothers have been medicine to many sick souls who were willing to swallow them whole: "You intended to harm me, but God intended it for good to accomplish what is now being done, the saving of many lives" (Genesis 50:20).

Take a good look at that word *intended*. It comes from the same Hebrew word translated "think" in Jeremiah 29:11: "For I know the thoughts that I think toward you, says the LORD, thoughts of peace and not of evil, to give you a future and a hope" (NKJV). God thinks of His children continually, and only in terms of what can be used toward our good, toward His plan for us, and toward the future. His intentions can only be pure. Right. Full of hope. Promoting peace.

Listen carefully. God did not haphazardly or accidentally let Joseph's brothers throw him in the pit. He had already considered it. Weighed it. Checked it against the plumb line of the plan. He had looked at the good it could ultimately accomplish, the lives that could be helped and even saved. Then, and only then, in His sovereign purpose, did He permit such harm to come to His beloved child. Had the incident not possessed glorious purpose, God would have disarmed it. Beloved, I don't just know this for a biblical fact; I know it for a personal fact. I live it every single day.

Can you think of anything more evil than child abuse? Anything at all? When I was a little girl, God already knew the plans He had for me . . . just like He knew the plans He had for you. In His sovereignty, He allowed a series of wrongs to come to me that had mammoth effects on my life. For many years, I reaped a whirlwind of negative consequences and added insult to injury by piling all manner of sin onto my victimization. Then one day, at the bottom of my pit, I raised my weary head and dirty, tear-streaked face to the sky. And redemption drew nigh. God knew the plans He had for me. Plans to prosper me and not to harm me. Plans to give me a hope and a future. I have lived long enough to see Him accomplish everything His Word says He will. Long enough to see beauty exceed the ashes and divine pleasure exceed the pain.

Dear one, whether or not I say a word about my past, God uses it every single day without fail in my ministry. In friendship. In motherhood. In marriage. He does the same for Keith. Perhaps the only thing worse than child abuse is the death of a child. In two separate incidents, Keith lost both his older brother and his younger sister. Day before yesterday, he spent an hour on the phone with a friend who'd lost her young adult brother in a freak car accident. He prayed for her and told her how he'd made it through the pain. He's done it a thousand times. Keith's past is part of who he is. And mine is part of who I am. Part of who God is making me.

Keith and I have been through so much—much more than we share with others—that, every now and then, the memories or regrets get one of us down. Last week Keith had one of those moments. We'd been discussing loved ones and their personality types. Were they sanguine, choleric, melancholy, or phlegmatic, or blends of two or more? He grew very serious and said, "What do you think I would have been like if all that hadn't happened? If Duke hadn't died. If my family hadn't had all those problems. If I hadn't been so messed up and turned to so much sin."

I believe the words that came out of my mouth were from God and not from me, because I wasn't smart enough or swift enough to think of them that fast. "Honey," I responded, "you're a much neater person *healed* than you would have been well."

Oh, beloved, you keep thinking about how things might have been had *that* not happened. Would you be willing to hear those same words I spoke to Keith? You have the capacity to be a ten times neater person healed than you would have been just plain well. Your wealth of experience makes you rich. Spend it on hurt people. They need it so badly. If God can use childhood abuse and family tragedy, He can use anything. You don't have to be in full-time ministry for Him to accomplish this kind of redemption. People in your workplace and your neighborhood are dying for hope. Dying to know there's a future. Dying to know there's a God . . . and that He's for them, not against them.

There's no telling what kind of bludgeon the enemy wanted to use against you and me, but in each of our lives, God has only allowed what He knew after much thought and deliberation could be used for good, for the helping—even saving—of many lives. Should you be willing to leave a legacy of faith, some of those lives you help will grace this earth after you're gone. Lives needing the kind of help you can give are surrounding you right now. Each one of them is worth the work.

God has given Keith and me the funniest daughters. Last year, Melissa was home for a few months between the end of college and the beginning of graduate school.

Maybe it's really kind of ridiculous that I never put alarm clocks in the girls' rooms when they were growing up. As sappy as this sounds, I wanted to wake them up myself. I wanted them to hear the voice of someone who loved them first thing in the morning.

Well, Melissa had been away to college for the most part of four years, but as any parent of adult children will tell you, they often lapse into their old patterns the second they slip back under their childhood covers. She had to go somewhere the next morning and asked me if I'd awaken her "like you used to, Mom." Yes, of course I would. And I did. The first time. The second time . . . The sixth time. The seventh time. She refused to get up. I finally raised my voice at her, and she responded, "Mom, get over here!" She threw back the covers of her bed, patted the fitted sheet, and said, "Lie down, Mom. Right here."

I balked. She pestered me until I sat down on the bed. "No, Mom! Lie all the way down. Get under the covers." I did. "Pull the covers up. Fluff your pillow up right under your head." I did. "Feel that bed, Mom." Oh, man, it felt good. Lying by my side in exactly the same posture, she looked over at me and quipped, "Now, would you want to get up if you were me?"

I've thought about that moment a thousand times. Life is hard. Most of us have reasons to lie down on life and never get up. In one way or another, at one time or another, by one person or another, each of us has been thrown into a pit. Most of us can rationalize staying angry, bitter, or fearful and insecure for the rest of our lives. We think we want people to lie down next to us, feel what we feel, and give us permission to stay there. But if they do, they help talk us into making ourselves at home in the early grave Satan dug for us. They agree to our living death.

Christ got down next to us in the grave, stayed the better part of three days, and then got up . . . so we'd have permission to get up too. And start living life.

Beloved, let this one sink in deeply: if God allowed you to be thrown into a pit, you weren't picked on; you were picked out. God entrusted that suffering to you because He has faith in you. Live up to it. All the way up.

3

When You Slip into a Pit

*Y*ou can slip in. That's the second way you can find yourself in a pit. Unlike the pit we get thrown in, we put ourselves into this one. But here's the catch: we didn't mean to. We just weren't watching where we were going. We got a little distracted, taken in by the new sights. The next thing we knew, we were in a hole, our feet ankle deep in mud.

You'd give anything if someone else had thrown you in, because you hate being the one to blame. In fact, at first you tried to think it was somebody else's fault. Anybody else's fault. But then you spent enough time in that pit for the noon sun to peak straight over your head. With eyes squinting and a hand cupped over your brow, you looked up to see the marks of two suspiciously familiar heels leaving twin ruts all the way from the mouth of the pit to where you're standing now. That sick feeling in your stomach tells you: nobody pushed you into this pit. You got yourself into this one. And you're not even sure how.

Right about now I wish we were sitting across from one another at the IHOP sharing stories. I'd get lemon crepes with a side of ham, and you could get the country omelet like Keith if you want to make me feel at home. But we'd hold off on ordering the coffee since there's a

Starbucks next door. Once at Starbucks, we'd talk till lunch, then we'd transfer our conversation to a nearby hole in the wall that serves the best cheese enchiladas in Houston. I bet you could widen my world considerably . . . and I yours. Not about food. About *pits*.

Haven't we both ended up in places we never meant to go? Can't we find fellowship in the suffering of slipping into a gosh-awful mess? Ironically, nothing makes us feel more alone than being in a pit, yet we have enough underground company to displace the overpopulation of West Texas gophers and leave them homeless for years. You just can't see all those underground neighbors because of your own pit wall. In case no one near you is 'fessing up, I'LL TALK LOUD. Sharing some lessons learned from those pits is the least I can do after the grace I've received.

I got a letter recently from a woman describing the terrible obstacles she faced. Then she proceeded to list all the wonderful things in my life and asked how someone like me had the audacity to offer advice (via Bible study) to someone like her. I didn't mind the question. She just didn't know. God has blessed me immeasurably but, to be sure, He has left some useful thorns and thistles in my yard to keep me from making myself at home in the fertilizer.

The sister who wrote me was right; she does have it tougher than I do. But I've lived long enough to know that no one has it easy. That Prada bag on someone's shoulder may look impressive, but it still holds junk. Every person deals with secret pain. Private hurts. Some of those aches have gone on for a long time. As graciously as I knew how, I wrote the woman back and included my own list. I'll spare you the gory details as long as you promise to trust that I do have a list.

I've given myself over to a season of deep despair only one time in my adult life. It was years ago, when I first faced up to my past. Recently I've been tempted to go there again. Tempted to take a break from fighting the good fight. Tempted to sit down in my difficulties, cry "Woe is me," and wallow for a while. But I know better. I've learned along the way that when Satan bartends, he prefers to serve mixed drinks. You know what I mean. Cocktails of troubles. Take them one at a time, and you can keep walking straight. Mixed all together, they can send you reeling. So I already know that if I give in to that temptation, this will be no quick-stop pity party. Satan has me registered at an extended-stay motel where I'm liable to slide from the front desk into the black hole in a split second. Nope. I'm not going into that pit. But let's just say I can see it from where I'm standing.

The whole thing started with a health issue that lasted for months and took a physical toll. The problem was finally resolved, but not without some forced alterations to my unreasonable schedule. Among other things, I had to admit my limitations and relinquish something I dearly love: a class I had taught for twenty-two years. I'd still like to be bitter about it, but I'm too scared of God. He's trying to help me out, and if I don't let Him, I'm liable to work myself into an early grave.

Perhaps very much like you, I also have a long-term relational situation that periodically—sometimes regularly—serves up some serious pain. I want the long-term situation to be fixed once and for all, but instead it stays put like a wart on a frog.

Frogs have been on my mind lately. We live near a pond that is home to a bellowing chorus of gargantuan green frogs. Somebody must have spiked the water with steroids, because these croakers are huge. Beanie found a dead one the other day and buried it in our backyard. Instead of decomposing like it should, the confounded thing must have petrified. Beanie keeps digging it up and burying it over and over again. It's driving me crazy.

That's how my relational challenge is. Just when I think what's causing the hurt is finally dead and buried, someone will dig it up. On a good day, I know God has entrusted it to me for the purpose of refining, humbling, and breaking me where I still need to be broken. It keeps me on my toes and down on my knees all at the same time. On a bad day, as Proverbs 13:12 says, my hope seems deferred and my heart feels sick.

At first glance, we might be tempted to think a pit of despair is not a pit of sin, but despair is not just sadness. It is hopelessness. We who have Christ possess the very essence—become the very embodiment—of hope (Romans 15:13). Hopelessness means we've believed the evil one's report over God's.

As my grandmother used to say, sometimes we need to give ourselves a good talking to. We need to speak straight to our soul where the problem resides and say something like this:

> Why are you downcast, O my soul?
> Why so disturbed within me?
> Put your hope in God,
> for I will yet praise him,
> my Savior and my God.
>
> (PSALM 42:5)

If we don't put our hope in God, we can talk ourselves into a pit. In the past twenty years of ministry, my ears have been privy to accounts of at least a thousand trips to the pit. As terrible as getting thrown into a pit can be, people never seem more frustrated and undone than when their slide into one is caused by their own ignorance or foolishness. Amid agonizing consequences, they are relentlessly haunted by what could have been avoided. Boy, do I know the feeling.

To get your wheels turning the right direction, I'll give you a handful of examples of ways you can slip into a pit. Mind you, a person doesn't have to go to some of the following extremes to end up in a pit. All a pit requires is that you feel stuck, that you feel you can't stand up effectively to your enemy, and that your vision is slowly failing. See if any of these examples come close to fitting you:

- You just meant to watch your weight. You certainly didn't intend to end up with an eating disorder. Nobody knows yet. Or at least, that's what you hope. You also hope you can stop all of this when you're thin enough.

- You just meant to borrow the money and pay every dime of it back. The interest was high, but you were on your way up the ladder. You never expected to be facing a mountain of debt that would throw you into bankruptcy.

- You just needed relief from your back pain so you could work. So you could enjoy your family again. You didn't intend to become addicted to prescription painkillers.

- You thought you'd finally made a really good friend. Found your soulmate. The last thing you intended was to end up in a lesbian relationship. Such a thing never entered your mind.

- Your sincerest heart's desire was to minister to that person. You weren't looking for the biggest entanglement of your life. How do you get out now? You know it's not healthy, but you hate to hurt the person. After all, for a while it worked for you as much as it did for her. Now you're being smothered to death.

- You were just doing business. I mean, it's a dog-eat-dog world out there, and you happen to be good at it. Sure, you knew the deal was a little "iffy," but you considered it creative financing. You certainly never meant to find yourself on a witness stand trying to avoid prison.

- You just meant to have a wonderful romance. After all, you'd waited so long as you watched so many other people fall in love. It was your turn. You wanted to plan a future with him. You didn't mean to fall into bed with him. Now you can't seem to fall out.

- You just meant to help your teenage son out of a few messes. Every time he seemed so repentant. Everybody needs second and third chances, someone to believe in him. You didn't tell his dad because your son begged you not to. Now your child is in a huge mess . . . and you have this sick feeling in your soul that you helped him get there.

- You just meant to flirt. It seemed harmless. He seemed happily married, and you were too. It was all in fun, you thought. Now you're in the biggest mess of your life.

- You just meant to have some privacy. You'd shared enough dorm rooms and apartments. You wanted to study. Hear yourself think. Never did it dawn on you that being by yourself might leave you lonely enough to look for company on the Web. Now it's gone someplace you didn't mean for it to go, and you can't seem to stop.

Of the three ways to get into a pit, I think the one I hate most is getting yourself into it. I hate the fool it makes of you. I also hate how the enemy uses the guilt over how you got into a pit to trap you into never getting out.

Hear me clearly: you cannot let him get away with that. Settle in your mind right now that staying in the pit is absolutely unacceptable. Lose it as an option. No matter how responsible and guilty you feel for sliding your way in, God wants you out. If you know Jesus Christ personally, you are not stuck. You do have the power to stand up against the enemy.

God still has a vision for you. His full intent is for you to live effectively (John 15:8) and abundantly (John 10:10). He loves you dearly, and the fact that you've been foolish doesn't diminish His love one single ounce.

This time, instead of giving yourself a good talking-to, use your mouth to talk to God. Echo the words of the psalmist when he cried:

> If I should say, "My foot has slipped,"
>   Your lovingkindness, O LORD, will
>   hold me up.

> When my anxious thoughts
> multiply within me,
> Your consolations delight my soul.
> (PSALM 94:18–19 NASB)

If you don't soak your brain in the truth that you are absolutely secure in the unchanging love of God, you will never feel worthy of getting out of the pit. Satan will keep your feet on slippery ground. When you want out of your pit, you have a golden opportunity to see the grace of God as you've never encountered it. Let God's loving-kindness hold you up, and ask Him to make His consolations your delight.

In some of the chapters that follow, we'll get more specific about how to get out of a pit, but for now I want you to concentrate on a gift you can bring out with you. Think of it as the door prize. Your plunder from the pit.

In every one of the scenarios I listed above, Satan used ignorance to get the person near enough to the mouth of the pit for him or her to slip in. One of the most priceless gifts we can bring out of our pit is newfound knowledge. Simply put, we can be a whole lot smarter coming out than we were going in. We are no longer innocent, but we have the opportunity before us to trade in our innocence for integrity. If we're willing, we can come out of the pit smartened up to Satan's agenda.

We can also tell on him to anyone who will listen. That's what I'm trying to do. When Scripture speaks of the Devil's schemes, it speaks of a well-contrived program based on a step-by-step progression (Ephesians 6:10–12). Though he tailors the specifics to fit individual weaknesses, I believe Satan's basic progressive plan remains consistent.

Distraction → Addiction → Destruction

Satan's definitive goal is to reap destruction, but distraction is usually his starting point. Scripture has a name for a small distraction that becomes a big distraction. It's called a *stronghold*. Scripture defines it as any and "every pretension that sets itself up against the knowledge of God" (2 Corinthians 10:5). Anything that becomes a bigger preoccupation in your mind than the truth and knowledge of God is a stronghold. In other words, if I have a relationship through which I can no longer prioritize Christ and His Word, Satan is building a stronghold there. If watching what I eat is no longer a means to better health and instead has become a major preoccupation, Satan is building a stronghold. If a same-sex friendship takes on a dimension of jealousy usually limited to a male-female romance, Satan is building a stronghold.

Get the picture? He has no intention of allowing the new focus to remain a simple distraction. The next step is addiction. An addiction is a highly effective way for something you *have* (a sin-induced problem) to turn into some place you *live* (a sin-induced pit). Defeat becomes a lifestyle. In Ephesians 4:18–19, the apostle Paul issued a strong warning to believers to no longer be like those who are "darkened in their understanding and separated from the life of God because of the ignorance that is in them due to the hardening of their hearts. Having lost all sensitivity, they have given themselves over to sensuality so as to indulge in every kind of impurity, with a continual lust for more."

What is true in the realm of sensuality is equally true in all other areas of repetitive sin. The present level of satisfaction will soon lose its sensitivity. We will need to indulge in more. Then a little more. In doing so, we become caught in the furious cycle of continual lust. That, my friend, is an addiction. Glance at the scripture again, because you don't want to miss the fact that it all started with ignorance. Even the people described in the verse, as rebellious as they may have been, drove into a pit beyond their original intention.

A person can be addicted to substances, behaviors, *and* relationships. (Many of us have learned all too painfully that emotional addictions can be as overwhelming as physical addictions.) But remember, addiction is not Satan's goal. Destruction is. He wants to destroy our lives, our callings, our sense of godly significance, our personal intimacy with God, and every relationship that matters to us. Yet if you belong to Christ, Satan cannot destroy *you*. The best he can do is to convince you that you're destroyed.

No, beloved, you're not. No matter what's happened. No matter how far you've gone. Wise up. The enemy is lying to you.

To wise up to Satan's progressive plan, we want to discern the early warning signals of a dangerous distraction and be on to him. Look back at the list of pit-slipping scenarios above, and you'll notice that many of them began innocently. Take the first five, for instance. It's not a sin to watch your weight. It's not a sin to get a loan. It's not a sin to seek relief from chronic physical pain that is robbing you of all quality of life. For crying out loud, it's certainly not a sin to make good friendships. And what does Christ want more than for us to minister to others? Somewhere along the way in each of these cases, Satan capitalized on an area of ignorance and detoured a healthy drive into a deep ditch.

My daughter Amanda made a good friend in college whom I have come to love as much as she does. Michelle is not only an avid lover of God, but she also can play a good, clean practical joke like no one I know. When she was at Texas A&M, she lived with some girlfriends in an apartment just a few doors down from four other buddies. She found the gullibility of these neighboring girls so delightfully inviting that she and her apartment mates contrived a plan. It began with swiping small things from their apartment. Knickknacks, vases, and the like. Just as Michelle hoped, they didn't notice. Soon she moved on to bigger and better things: small pictures, flower arrangements, and so on. Again, not a word. She progressed to obvious things like taking a framed picture off the wall. She grinned ear to ear with accomplishment when she recalled the coup de grâce: dragging one of their breakfast-room chairs right out from under their noses. The unsuspecting victims never said a word.

Beside themselves with victory, Michelle and her roommates soon invited their neighbors to join them for dinner. The décor was arranged to make them feel right at home. Every knickknack was displayed. Every framed picture in open view. The flower arrangement on the table. And at the very head of the table? Ah, yes: the victory chair.

We laughed our heads off as Michelle described the looks on their friends' faces as the light dawned. Their eyes jumped from one thing to another like the steel ball in a pinball machine. They looked at each other and then at their hosts, chirping madly, "Hey, that's mine!"

You gotta love it. Till somebody who hates you does it. Somebody sinister. Somebody who does it for a living. You and I have to be on to the enemy's schemes when he swipes the first knickknack and make an immediate adjustment. For example, when you realize a relationship you've just begun is going to be destructive, you can bow out before you get any closer. Or if you realize your job places you in a virtually undetectable position to use money, and you're in a financially vulnerable situation right now, set up safeguards and automatic accountability. Live out in the light. Don't just practice innocence. Practice integrity.

The last thing God wants is for you and me to live in fear. Undoubtedly "the one who is in you [the Holy Spirit] is greater than the one who is in the world [Satan]" (1 John 4:4). We don't want to be afraid, but we must be alert. If you're in Christ, you have a built-in alarm system. Like my buddy Vicky's pacemaker, which one day sounded an alarm from inside of her when the battery was going out, the Holy Spirit is in us, and if we don't quench Him, He'll tell us early on when we're headed for trouble. He'll also tell us whether to be careful right where we are or to bail out altogether.

The hardest part may be that you won't always understand why the beeper is going off—why God is directing you to back off from a situation or a relationship. When this happens, beware of rationalizing yourself into a pit! Mind what the Holy Spirit is telling you, even if you don't know why. You may live on for years without clear understanding, but you can praise God by faith, knowing He veered your car a different direction to keep you out of some kind of ditch.

Another way you can sometimes recognize Satan at work is that you begin to feel backed into a corner. If a new relationship or opportunity is causing you to feel trapped, God could be flagging you that Satan is all over it. God issues dos and don'ts, but always for freedom's sake. Psalm 18:36 says of our God, "You enlarge my steps under me, and my feet have not slipped" (NASB). Satan backs us into a corner on slippery ground strategically close to the nearest pit. God enlarges our steps under us, enabling us to see a pit from a greater distance so we don't have to live in constant dread of falling into another one.

When my daughter Melissa was a senior in high school, Satan plotted her path right into a pit and steered her toward it. She was a slim and darling size 6 before a series of unhappy incidents caused her some deep sadness. She lost her appetite and dropped down to a size 2. At one point she could even wear a size 0. Mind you, she was 5'8". (Incidentally, the thinner she got, the more affirmation she got from her peers.)

The nightmare didn't start with an eating issue, but it certainly ended up there. Keith and I were scared half to death. We sought God with everything we had, received godly counsel, prayed scriptures over her, and fought the enemy ferociously. After a few excruciating months, Melissa came to a place where she wanted out of that pit. She called upon her God relentlessly, and He came to her rescue. Melissa emerged from that pit with a gift: she couldn't get enough of God's Word. Her ticket out turned into her soul's delight. Scriptures that seem as old and familiar as a worn-out bathrobe to some people came totally alive to Melissa.

One day she called me and blurted, "Are you ready for this?" I grinned, sat back, and replied, "Hit me."

"Mother, did you know that God prepares a table before me in the presence of my enemy?" Her newfound passion had obviously led her to the Twenty-Third Psalm. "And get this," she bubbled. "He forces my enemy to watch as He anoints my head with oil!" The enemy had gotten one over on Melissa. She was ecstatic to be getting one over on him.

Beloved, listen up a minute. God prepares a table before you in the presence of your enemy too. And guess what? It can be decorated and surrounded by every single knickknack, vase, flower arrangement, and picture Satan stole from your place. You can sit right down in that chair—the one he dragged out of your house right under your nose. And don't you get up from that chair until God anoints you with an overflow of the Holy Spirit that only comes to those most desperate for Him. Right in front of your enemy's eyes.

Look at it this way: the fact that you are reading this book—or anything like it—betrays that Satan didn't take you anywhere near the finish line he planned for you. When you slipped into that pit, you went to a place you never intended. Now you're going to a place *Satan* never intended. Don't you stop until the enemy is sorry he ever messed with you.

4

When You Jump into a Pit

*Y*ou can jump in. That's the third and final way you can land in a pit. Before you take the plunge, you can be well aware that what you're about to do is wrong, probably even foolish. But for whatever reason, the escalating desire to do it exceeds the good sense not to, and you've hauled off and jumped square into the bull's-eye.

Don't start squirming and think I'm about to talk down to you—believe me, I've jumped into my share of pits—but I'd like to ask your permission to talk straight to you. If I don't tell it like it really is, you'll just tune out what I have to say like you've tuned out countless others who said the same thing, but so properly that you ignored them. I know how that is.

So I'm going to try a different approach. If I didn't care, I would save myself the trouble. After all, by nature I'm a people pleaser. The thing is, I now know what I needed at my own times of pit-jumping, and few people in my life had the guts to give it. I also happen to know that if jumping in a pit is your *modus operandi*, you're probably cynical enough not to respect me if I don't spit it out.

In fact (and, mind you, I'm still talking straight, not down), if you are a confirmed pit-jumper, you probably have a pretty serious authority problem overall. Forgive my amateur psychology, but my guess is that your primary authority figure was, or is, either a wimp or a fraud. God is neither. He knows what it will take to get your attention, and He's willing to do it. Trust me. I know this from personal experience. I also know the games we play with one another as we make excuses for our gross inconsistencies. Especially we churchy types. So, if you don't mind, I'll get to the point.

When all is said and done, you, like me, probably do what you do because you want to. You ordinarily jump in a pit because you like the trip. It looks good. It feels good. Or it tastes good. It just doesn't last nearly long enough, which is why we come back and take the next trip.

Stay with me here, beloved. Surely you know that it takes one to know one. The only reason I'm not still in a pit is because, after many warnings, God mushroomed such devastating consequences of sin and emotional unhealthiness that it nearly killed me—did kill the old me, as a matter of fact. As Job 33:29–30 says:

> God does all these things to a man—
> twice, even three times—
> to turn back his soul from the pit,
> that the light of life may shine on him.

God brought me to a place where I was willing to do anything to get out of the pit and everything to stay out. To be out of the mud and mire and have my feet upon a rock became what I wanted more than anything in the world. If you have the same tendency toward pit-jumping, I wish more than anything to talk you into crying out for deliverance before you reach the point I did. Before your world as you know it comes tumbling down. Praise God, He is the rebuilder of ruins, but surely there are easier ways to get a new home than to let an emotional tornado tear the old one to pieces.

What if a domestic tornado didn't have to huff and puff and blow your house down to get your attention? What if, before the bottom fell out, you would respond to a Voice in the wilderness saying, "Stop it!" (see Isaiah 1:16)? And what if that same Voice—the only One that matters—was willing to tell you how to stop?

If we were willing to let it, it would happen. God in His tender mercy gives us plenty of warnings enabling us to avoid pits, but the problem with us pit-jumpers is that we don't want to hear those warnings. We want what we want. So we stick our fingers in our ears before we jump in.

What on earth drives us to do such a thing? Of all the ways into the pit, jumping in is by far the most dangerous and the most supremely—oh, that I had an even stronger word!—*consequential*. You see, motive is huge to God. So is character. Primarily His character, which we are created to emulate. And He will not be mocked. The very segment of Scripture where we're told that God won't be mocked is strategically centered in the context of reaping what we sow (Galatians 6:7–9). We can't fool Him by hiding our inner motive. God looks intently not only at what we've done and how, but also at *why* we did it. First Chronicles 28:9 says, "The LORD searches every heart and understands every motive behind the thoughts."

Do you want to hear something ironic? This very aspect of God (His omniscience) that helps save our scrawny necks when we've slipped into a pit nearly hangs us when we've jumped into it. If you've ever made that jump, I really don't have to tell you that you had your reasons. I'll just throw out a token few common reasons here for good measure. Maybe you can find your own somewhere on the list. A pit-jumper . . .

- Meant to cheat the company
- Wanted to go to bed with that person
- Set out to take vengeance
- Went into that relationship knowing full well that person was an unbeliever . . . or had a dark side
- Wanted to get drunker than a skunk. Higher than a kite. Lower than a snake's belly.

You get the picture. Psalm 19:13 gives a couple of names to pit-jumping. Facing his own bent for jumping into pits, the psalmist pled with God:

Keep Your servant from willful sins;
do not let them rule over me.
Then I will be innocent,
and cleansed from blatant rebellion. (HCSB)

Willful sins. Blatant rebellion. The two are as tied together as a bird and a feather. Innate in every act of rebellion is an authority figure we're rebelling against.

You and I are never going to be able to submit to authority perfectly as long as our feet of clay are stuck to planet Earth. But don't let anybody talk you into thinking you can't be liberated from willful sin and blatant rebellion just because he or she hasn't been. I know for a fact that you can be completely set free from every sin that rules over you. Then and only then will you and I possess the kind of innocence possible for *Homo sapiens* still inhaling terrestrial air. To get there, we not only need some deep repentance (in essence, a change of mind resulting in a change of direction), we need some marrow-deep healing, or we'll simply change right back.

I stumbled onto a name for our problem just recently while perusing a commentary on James 1:13–15. Before we delve into that name, a fresh reading of the scripture wouldn't hurt us, so I'll start there:

When tempted, no one should say, "God is tempt-ing me." For God cannot be tempted by evil, nor does he tempt anyone; but each one is tempted when, by his own evil desire, he is dragged away and enticed. Then, after desire has conceived, it gives birth to sin, and sin, when it is full-grown, gives birth to death.

The original Greek word translated "evil desire" is *epithumia*. Actually, the word is neutral and can be used for right desires as well as wrong ones. The context, as in James 1:14, determines whether or not the desire is wrong. And in this Scripture segment, the *New American Commentary* defines *epithumia* as "deformed desire."

That's what I had. Deformed desire. In my own pit-jumping (as opposed to pit-slipping), I often ended up doing exactly what I set out to do . . . what at that moment or in that season I thought I *wanted* to do. Like you, perhaps, I wished I didn't want the things I did. I often hated what I wanted. Still, desire—deformed and destructive—lurched and led.

One of the most important shifts in my belief system began with the realization that I had a messed-up "want to." I had thought of my heart as only sinful. I didn't realize that, deeper still, my heart was sick.

I'm not the only one. I have a good friend who graciously invited me into her harrowingly self-destructive mind. After spending ninety days in jail for a second DUI, she expressed to me that the whole time she was there, she never had any other plan than to walk out that door and get a drink. She reasoned that the only thing she needed to do differently was perhaps not drive.

After getting out, she got too drunk to keep her appointments with her probation officer and ended up spending a third gig behind bars, this time for six months. A few days after release? Same thing.

In light of all she'd lost—self-respect, job, marriage, kids—her walking out the door and doing the same thing again baffled me. I asked her why she had done it. Hadn't the relentless demand of her internal organs finally had time to die down? She said dryly, "Because I wanted to. Beth, I don't think you're listening. I wanted to drink. I liked how it made me feel."

Or how it made her *not* feel.

The desire to *not* desire is one of the most deformed desires we'll ever have. One of the biggest mistakes we could ever make is to assume that the goal for godly people is to not feel. Nothing could be further from the truth. We were created out of holy passion *for* holy passion. So perfectly fitted for passion are we that we will find it one way or another. If we don't find it in Christ, we'll find it in things like lust, anger, and greed.

Never minimize the power of desire. Though doing what you need to do is the place to start, you'll never make it in the long haul motivated by need alone. The most self-disciplined among us may walk in victory for a few weeks out of our need to do the right thing, but it will rarely carry us to the finish line. Each of us will ultimately do what we want to do.

Is it any wonder that the first words of Christ recorded in the incomparable gospel of John are "What do you want?" Hear Him echo the same words to you today. "What do *you* want, child?" What are your secret desires? Place them before Him. Name every single one. No matter how healthy or unhealthy. No matter how respectable. No matter how deformed. I am proof that God can heal the most messed up "want to."

In recent years no verse has meant more to me than Psalm 40:8: "I delight to do Your will, O my God; Your Law is within my heart" (NASB). I still can hardly fathom that I can say those words and mean them after where I've been. God healed my deformed desires, finally getting through my thick skull that the things He wanted for me were the best things life could offer. Using the hammer of His Word and the anvil of His unfailing love, God reshaped my disfigured desires until what I wanted more than anything on earth was what He wanted. Somewhere along the way, God's "law" transferred from the stone tablets of my head to the soft tissue of my heart. I bought in—not just spiritually, but emotionally. Jesus finally, completely, won my heart. And not just mine. Remember my good friend who wanted that next drink regardless of the consequences? I've never known anyone in more bondage.

Christ finally got through to her, won her heart, and changed her desires. She's a miracle. I'm a miracle. If He can deliver the two of us, He can deliver anyone.

So much of our propensity toward pit-jumping springs from the fact that somewhere down deep inside, we just don't trust God. We think He's like all the others who have cheated or betrayed us. As my friend Chris Thom says, "God is not just a big us." Like Adam and Eve, we let the enemy taunt us into believing God is holding out on us. Our drive for the proverbial forbidden fruit is our innate belief that what we are denied is exactly what we want most.

Satan was a liar then, and he's a liar now.

God doesn't just say no because it makes Him feel good about Himself. God feels fine about Himself. He doesn't need us to feel small so He can feel big—He's huge. He doesn't have to be bossy to feel like the boss—He's the Master of the universe. If God forbids something, the sooner we believe and confess that it's for our sakes, the better off we'll be.

In my research for this book, I learned that certain kinds of relationships and people become automatic pits for us the second we intimately engage. A relationship that is so enticing to us precisely because it's forbidden is nothing but a decoratively painted door to a cavernous pit.

Proverbs 23:27 says that "a prostitute is a deep pit; an adulteress is a narrow well" (ESV). The King James

Version uses a far stronger word than "prostitute"—and one that suggests that the term isn't limited to someone who is paid to have sex. It refers to anyone who sleeps around and practices immorality as a virtual lifestyle. The verse is equally true in gender reversal. A man who sleeps around is a deep pit, and an adulterer is a narrow well. Mess with them and, in a manner of speaking, you'll hurl yourself in the bowels of the earth with such meteoric force that only God can pull you out. I don't care how flattering someone's attention may be. If he or she is immoral or married to somebody else, an intimate relationship of any kind with that person will automatically—not probably or eventually—hurl you into a pit. ETA? Instantly.

Based on everything the Word of God says and everything I've experienced, heard, or observed, I promise you that forbidden relationships never turn out well. Let me say that one more time: *never.* The pit is deep and dark. And before you know it, you'll find that you are in it all alone.

I've also lived long enough and listened hard enough to become convinced that we are almost always right when we get a nagging feeling somewhere down inside that a person to whom we're growing increasingly attached has a serious dark side. That's the Holy Spirit warning us. Learn to associate darkness with a pit. I say all of this to you out of deep love and concern. Repent and run.

Automatic pit-jumping has a far broader range than matters of sexuality. Forbidden sexual relationships simply trigger some of the boldest scriptural guarantees of disaster. The wider context is anything that God goes to the trouble to forbid.

He's actually a "yes" kind of God (2 Corinthians 1:20). You can mark this one down any time and every time: God's "no" is a quick shove away from a pit. The sooner the shove, the better.

I didn't begin to live in victory just because all opportunity to jump finally disappeared. While I was still at greatest risk, God stayed on me, worked with me, and built trust in me until finally I'd go where He pointed. That's been our MO for a while, but He's wise to never let me forget the excruciating pain of where I've been . . . lest I be tempted to go back. Until we're nine-tenths in the grave, none of us is past the danger of a pit.

Get a load of the words out of King David's mouth immediately after promising God he'd lead a blameless life: "When will you come to me?" (Psalm 101:2). Translation? "I don't know how long I can keep this up. Are You coming soon? Killing me soon?" Can't we pit-jumpers relate? Quick carnal impulses leap into our heads at times, but once we've let God win our hearts, a high tide of holy desire can come and wash them away like jellyfish swept from the shore.

Recently, at a speaking engagement, a group of

women gave me a Barbie. It wasn't the first. I think the joke started after I told the story of my young friend Savannah, who often sits with me at church. She's a grown-up eleven now, but when she was about six and seven, she loved to bring her Barbies to church. I'm happy to say that she dressed them in their more modest outfits. Of course, there was that one time when a skirt was so short I had to wrap an offering envelope around her hips. (I had to remind myself that sanctification is a process, and some Barbies need extra time for change to become observable. I was one of them.)

As long as Savannah's Barbies were at church, I surmised they might as well engage in worship, so she and I either held them in front of us where they could face the worship team or propped them against the back of the pew. Either way, we always lifted up their hands. Since their mouths wouldn't open and their knees wouldn't bend, we felt hand-lifting to be our only recourse. Barbie elbows don't bend either, so their praise was highly demonstrative for our conservative congregation.

Somehow the large group with whom I shared the Barbie account found it amusing, and the theme caught on. I've been receiving Barbies ever since.

This most recent Barbie was dressed like me (hip, I hope, but alas, modest). She had a makeshift Bible in one hand (appeared to be a King James) while the other was stretched decisively heavenward. This doll had one inadvertent similarity to me that overrode all the others. It even made up for the gross age discrepancy no one seemed willing to acknowledge. One of Barbie's feet had been gnawed right off at the calf. The group extended their regrets, of course, explaining that the family dog of the original owner had gotten hold of the doll the day before they left. But they decided the doll was, by and large, no worse for the wear.

I stared at the Barbie for a minute. She looked so strange at first. So well-coiffed, so fitted for her calling, and yet she had a gnawed-off foot. Then I nodded. Not to anyone else really. Just to God. Well, maybe also to Barbie. Though the group didn't know it, they'd hit the nail right on the head, or maybe the leg right on the stump. That was me all right.

No, I don't have a missing leg, but if you could see me with your spiritual eyes, surely at least one of my legs is gnawed off at the knee. Ephesians 4:27 warns, "Do not give the devil a foothold." Uh, too late. Satan has wounded me, but he hasn't devoured me. He got the leg, but he's never gotten the thigh, though goodness knows he wanted it. I may walk with a spiritual limp, but thanks be to God, who holds me up and urges me to lean on Him, at least I can walk. So can you. Walk away from that pit before it's the death of you.

With love, Beth.

≈ 5 ≈

Getting Out of
Your Pit

*Y*ou can get out. Regardless of whether you were thrown in, you slipped in, or you jumped in, you can get out. We don't need to deal with our pits. We need to get out of our pits.

You can do it. Even if you have a history of failed attempts. Even if you don't think you deserve it. Even if you've never lived anywhere else. But here's the catch: you can't get yourself out. Remember the number-one characteristic of a pit? Mud and mire. The quicksand kind that gulps your feet whole. Try as you may, you will never successfully pull yourself out of a pit. Somebody else has to come to your rescue. You can opt for human help or you can opt for God.

God meant for people to offer one another a helping hand. The trouble comes when we insist upon someone equally human becoming our deliverer. Another person—rare though he may be—can pull us out of a pit but, for the life of him, he can't set us free.

Take Joseph, for instance. While he was kicking and screaming in the waterless bottom of his pit, his brothers looked up from their picnic lunch and

saw a caravan of Ishmaelites coming from Gilead. Their camels were loaded with spices, balm and myrrh, and they were on their way to take them down to Egypt. Judah said to his brothers, "What will we gain if we kill our brother and cover up his blood? Come, let's sell him to the Ishmaelites and not lay our hands on him; after all, he is our brother, our own flesh and blood." His brothers agreed. So when the Midianite merchants came by, his brothers pulled Joseph up out of the cistern and sold him for twenty shekels of silver to the Ishmaelites, who took him to Egypt.

(GENESIS 37:25–28)

Agreed, getting sold into slavery was a far better option than starving to death in a cistern. But a kind soul will give the brothers too much credit for their compassion without Psalm 105:18 to round out the picture. We're told that the Ishmaelites "bruised his feet with shackles, his neck was put in irons."

Don't forget, Joseph was only seventeen. Pampered and spoiled at that. He'd probably never even made up his pallet in the morning. Suddenly, he was a slave in shackles heading who knows where.

Scripture leaves no doubt that the sovereignty of God was in full pendulum swing, directing every detail from Canaan to Egypt for the common good. Years passed, however, before Joseph began to grasp the work of his true Deliverer. In our relational parallel, if a man—or woman—pulls us out of the pit, solely assuming the role of deliverer, he or she will inadvertently sell us into slavery of one kind or another almost every time.

Ancient Israel found herself scrambling for help as she faced imminent takeover by the massive army of the Assyrians. God could have thwarted the assault in a blink of His holy eye, but stayed His hand, awaiting their cry of repentance. Yet the people "would have none of it" (Isaiah 30:15). Rather than humble themselves and do what was required for true protection and restoration, Israel preferred calling upon the Egyptians for protection. They slapped a coat of gloss over their past and decided Egypt wasn't all that bad. Particularly when compared to the threatening Assyrians. Isaiah 30 records God's response:

> "Woe to the obstinate children,"
>> declares the LORD,
>> "to those who carry out plans that
>>> are not mine,
>> forming an alliance, but not by my
>>> Spirit,
>> heaping sin upon sin;
> who go down to Egypt
>> without consulting me;
>> who look for help to Pharaoh's
>>> protection,
>> to Egypt's shade for refuge.

> But Pharaoh's protection will be to your
> shame,
>> Egypt's shade will bring you
>> disgrace. . . .
> Everyone will be put to shame
>> because of a people useless to
>> them."
>
> (vv. 1–3, 5)

Israel didn't need Egypt. She needed God. At his best, man can make a mighty fine man, but he's a useless god. The job's too big for him.

Effective deliverance takes the ability to read people's minds, because what we say often doesn't match where we are. Only God can hang with us through the length and depth of our need. And our baloney. Whether or not I realized it, I usually found a way to frame my pit to make me look like a victim. Not only is God omniscient, His Word is "sharper than any double-edged sword", cutting our baloney so thin He can see straight through it. He knows when we're kidding others. He knows when we're kidding ourselves.

Knowing all we are, all we feel, and all we hide, God overflows with love and willingness to deliver us. Even after Israel sought the help of the Egyptians, inviting the chastisement of God, Isaiah 30 testified, "Yet the LORD longs to be gracious to you; he rises to show you compassion" (v. 18).

Longs to be gracious. I like the ring of that. We're also repeatedly told that "His love endures forever," which means the Lord is gracious for *long*. That's what former pit-dwellers like me must have. We need a Deliverer who is in for the long haul. Philippians 1:6 tells us that God, who began a good work, is faithful to complete it. Frankly, work doesn't get harder than pit-dweller pulling. True delivery takes some time, some titanic effort, and more patience than the best of people possess. You and I need a strong arm and a long arm.

The apostle Paul described God's tenacity in 2 Corinthians 1:10 when he said, "He *has* delivered us . . . he *will* deliver us. On him we have set our hope that he will *continue* to deliver us" (emphasis mine). Past. Present. Future. That's the kind of deliverance you and I are looking for. We need a lifetime warranty. The "Sovereign LORD" alone is "my strong deliverer" (Psalm 140:7). Everybody else will wear out. They may pull us out of that pit and even hang around a while to push us away when we try to get right back in it. But eventually their backs will give out. And when they do, we're liable to be mad at them. They let us down.

A dear sister in Christ came to me grieving the loss of a friendship. She described how her friend had been there for her through a difficult time. In fact, she'd never have made it without her. They'd talked for hours. Gotten so tight. She'd become the closest confidant my sister in Christ had ever had.

Over time her friend seemed a little less attentive. Less warm. Less patient. Or was she just imagining things? After all, she was still polite. Then she took longer to return her calls. She'd hear that her friend was doing things they used to do with someone else. It hurt her feelings. She tried to talk to her about it. Her friend hugged her and said all was well and she loved her. I have no doubt she did. She just couldn't keep carrying her. Before long, she quit calling altogether.

Does this scenario sound familiar? If you can't relate, I can relate enough for both of us. And from both sides. I'm sure I've worn people out, and I've been worn out. A fellow human may have initially pulled us out of a pit, but somewhere along the way, he or she accidentally sold us into the slavery of nearly debilitating disappointment. When it happens, we reason that we might as well have stayed in the pit.

Tragically, countless relationships end exactly this way. I wouldn't for a minute minimize the pain of a relationship broken by unsustainable expectations. I've knelt with too many weeping women at the altar of my church sanctuary, only to learn that they needed prayer over feelings deeply hurt by someone sitting elsewhere in that room. When such a close, dependable relationship is injuriously severed, the knife penetrates to the exact depth we've invited that friend or mentor into our private lives. Indeed, one of the primary reasons we're so wounded is because the person knew what we were going through and still abandoned us.

What I'm about to say can be painful to hear, but I pray that God will use it toward someone's healing: sometimes a person abandons us not in spite of what we're going through, but directly because of it. If our helping friends actually did something that overtly wronged us, they bear responsibility before God for that. But if they wronged us only by running out of fuel and dropping out of the struggle, we might need to realize they've done all they felt they could humanly do, and let them go without bitterness or anger.

A few particularly faithful pit-pullers may genuinely try to hang with it for a while. For months. Even years. If they don't seem to complain much, maybe the process is feeding something unhealthy in them too. You may reason that at least they didn't sell you off into slavery. Oh, yes they did. The world has a name for this caravan: *codependency.* The only difference between the two scenarios is that, in this one, they jumped on the wagon to Egypt with you.

The autumn Melissa headed off to college, my buddy Bonita and I got the harebrained idea to take golf lessons. With empty nests, we thought for sure we'd have time for a hobby. What idiots. And of all hobbies, why golf? I don't like the outfits, and I certainly don't like the shoes. I don't like how you have to be quiet when other people swing. And I don't think your body is supposed to twist that way either. It's not natural. Furthermore, it's hot outside in the summer. Especially three doors from Hades where I live.

I hate golf. But I like a few golfers, which is exactly how we got into this mess. I reckon we were trying to impress our husbands by thinking of something we could do together . . . like they were really going to shoot eighteen holes with us. Our men were wise enough to forgo our offer for them to teach us to play. Knowing that neither marriage could have stood the strain, they dropped the cash for someone else to do it. A real, live golf pro.

I could tell the first day he didn't like us. I don't know what his problem was: perhaps he had a mean mother. Could we help it if the woman in the pro shop was still ringing up our new accessories when he was ready to start the lesson?

"Do we bring our purses?"

He just stared at us, so we guessed not.

After finding a locker, we finally made our way to the golf cart for our quick zip to the putting green. Wearing our best southern manners, Bonita and I could hardly get in the cart for insisting that the other take the front seat alongside the driver. "No, by all means, you sit up there!"

The pro curtly suggested that we sit down and get on our way. Then he hit a speed bump and our new sunglasses fell off. Looking back now, I suspect foul play. I'm nearly certain he was trying to throw *us* off.

Nevertheless, our spirits could not be dampened. Every time one of us hit the golf ball, the other one clapped. With boundless enthusiasm, I'd cheer, "Bonita, that was so good!" Then I'd putt and, good friend that she is, she'd return the affirmation. "Ah, Beth! Now, that was *really* good!" Finally, the golf pro had heard enough. He darted his eyes back and forth between us almost like he was having a seizure, waved his arms, and said, "Neither one of you is any good!"

That was my last golf lesson. It's a shame, I know, but who has the patience for a golf pro who obviously overlooks his morning devotionals? I tried to remind myself to pray for his mother.

Sometimes we latch onto someone for dear life who is no better off than we are. I believe strongly in support groups, but somebody in that group better be on the upside looking in. Preferably way up. Otherwise, we're liable to keep cheering back and forth, "That was so good!" when, in reality, none of us is doing well. If we keep patting each other on our broken backs, how will they ever mend? Christ asked the question more effectively in Luke 6:39: "Can the blind guide the blind? Shall they not both fall into a pit?" (ASV).

In case you need to come up for air, let's switch sides for a minute. Not only has each of us searched for a human deliverer, we've also tried to become a deliverer to someone else. I could offer an embarrassing number of personal examples, but I'll settle for one.

A couple of years ago, a pit-dwelling loved one (not my husband or daughters) charged me with gallivanting all over the country to help others but not caring about her. The deeper she sunk in her pit, the deeper she became buried in her resentment.

Her accusation that I didn't care couldn't have been further from the truth. Though I'd never thrown myself into her plight no holds barred, I loved her dearly and had tried countless times to help. Still, her resentment cut me to the quick. So I made a decision to do whatever it took to turn this woman around.

Two months later, we were both in shambles. She was mad at me, and I was mad at her. Not speaking, as a matter of fact. I am thankful that we got over it, but the experience settled something that had always nagged at me: even if we are unselfish and undistracted enough to give another person our all for an indefinite period of time, can we save them from themselves? I don't think so.

Does this mean we shouldn't get involved with hurting people? Not at all! We may be hopelessly inadequate as deliverers for one another, but never think for a moment we can't be used of God to effect profound change in someone's life.

We can have a tremendous impact over a life in the pit. First of all, we can impact pit-dwellers by example.

We can show them that living outside the pit is possible by living that way ourselves.

Second, we can impact pit-dwellers by prayer. Second Corinthians 1:10–11 adds this concerning God's past, present, and future deliverance of His children: "On him we have set our hope that he will continue to deliver us as *you help us by your prayers*" (emphasis mine). We have a God-given invitation—if not responsibility—to join the process of someone's divine deliverance from peril or pit.

Third, we can impact pit-dwellers by encouragement. Hebrews 3:13 calls us to "encourage one another daily . . . that none of you may be hardened by sin's deceitfulness." Satan has a tremendous investment in convincing a person that, with his or her track record, sustainable victory is impossible. That's a lie. Say so.

Fourth, we can impact pit-dwellers by doggedly directing them to Jesus. Like the men carrying the paralytic on the mat, do everything you can to "lay [the person] before Jesus" (Luke 5:18). Keep telling her who the true Deliverer is. Keep pointing her toward the only One who will not let her down.

Fifth, to the degree that God has developed biblical wisdom in us, we can impact pit-dwellers through our advice and counsel. Sometimes it doesn't take a professional to give good advice, but when it does, I am a huge proponent of godly professional counseling. Got it myself, and I'm not sure where I'd be without it. When someone brings me an issue way out of my league, I'm going to stay on her like a bird dog on point until she goes to counseling or seeks professional advice.

Yet even the best of godly counselors have to guard against their counselees setting them up as deliverers. All of us were born with a natural tendency to attach ourselves to a savior and worship him. To see him high and lifted up. That's why it had better be Christ. We are safe with no other. Isaiah 43:11 says it succinctly: "I, even I, am the LORD, and apart from me there is no savior."

Maybe this chapter wasn't meant so much for you. Maybe you can't think of a single time you made someone else responsible for your happiness . . . your wholeness . . . your healing. Then again, maybe some of the fog has cleared on a relationship you believed at one time would be a deliverance of sorts for you. Maybe you're beginning to see that this person wasn't being heartless and hateful when they dropped the rope. Just human. Maybe you can allow God to bring you to the place to forgive that person for failing to be Jesus for you. Or maybe you should fire someone who still insists on trying. Maybe you—like me—can now forgive yourself for accidentally setting someone up for failure. Maybe that someone was you. And maybe both of us could just let Jesus be Jesus.

6

The Three Steps Out of Your Pit

*Y*ou can opt for God. Pitching every other plan, thanks-but-no-thanks to every other deliverer, you can opt for God.

The beautiful thing about opting for God is that you are opting for everything He brings. Because He is infinite, you will never reach the end of all He offers of Himself. Nothing on earth is like fully engaging with God. *Nothing.*

If you're willing to engage God as your deliverer from the pit, the full-throttle relationship you develop with Him will be the most glorious thing that has ever happened to you. Far more glorious than the deliverance itself. You will find thankfulness in your heart for every person who let you down, for ultimately, their failure set you up for this most ecstatic relationship you will ever experience.

If you're willing. You may end up closing this book after what you read in the next fifteen seconds, but should you decide to take the challenge, beloved, you are on your way out of that pit. Here's the challenge: God wants everything you've got. Uncontested priority. Every egg in one basket. All your weight on one limb. This very moment He has His fingers gripped on your chin, saying, *Right here, child. Look right here. Don't look right or left. Stare straight into My face. I am your Deliverer. There is none like Me.*

God will be your complete Deliverer or nothing at all. That's the one rule of divine rescue. This I can tell you from both Scripture and experience: God absolutely refuses to share His glory. Anyone who shares His position as deliverer in your life is sharing His glory. God won't stand for that. He may use any number of people in your life to come alongside and encourage you as part of His process. But He alone must deliver you . . . or you will never be free.

With that one unwavering rule established, let's get busy. To get where we want to go, we need a comprehendible, biblical how-to. I believe the Bible proposes three steps out of the pit, and each involves your mouth:

- Cry out
- Confess
- Consent

Let's take a look at each step. Our part of the process begins and extends in a very specific action described in Psalm 40, a portion of the Scripture that became the inspiration for this book:

> I waited patiently for the LORD;
>> he turned to me and heard my cry.
> He lifted me out of the slimy pit,

out of the mud and mire;
he set my feet on a rock
and gave me a firm place to stand.
(VV. 1–2)

In this passage, the pit-dweller's deliverance began with a cry. Weeping may accompany this cry, but tears alone mean little. You've probably heard the saying: "Sentimentality is no indication of a warm heart. Nothing weeps more copiously than a chunk of ice." We can cry our eyes out over the pain of our situation and still refuse to change. Those kinds of tears often flow from our desperation for *God* to change and our frustration that He won't. If you're like me, sometimes you want Him to bend the rules for you and bless your disobedience or half-heartedness.

His refusal to bend to our will may at first seem uncompassionate in light of all we've endured, but He's pushing for the best thing that will ever happen to us. God will never be codependent with you. He wants you up on your feet, living abundantly, profoundly, effectively. And it all begins with a cry.

The kind the psalmist was talking about erupts from the deepest part of a person's soul as if his or her life depends on it. This cry from the depths makes its first good use of the pit, aiming the petition straight up those narrow walls to the throne of God as if shot like fireworks from the cylinder of a Roman candle.

You will be hard pressed to find a more repetitive concept in Scripture than God's intervention coming as a direct response to someone crying out. Here are a few samples pulled like fish from a sea full of them:

- "He will deliver the needy who cry out" (Psalm 72:12).
- "He took note of their distress when he heard their cry; for their sake he remembered his covenant and out of his great love he relented" (Psalm 106:44–45).
- "The LORD is a refuge for the oppressed, a stronghold in times of trouble. . . . He does not ignore the cry of the afflicted" (Psalm 9:9, 12).
- "I love the LORD, for he heard my voice; he heard my cry for mercy." (Psalm 116:1).

Why does the process start with our cry? Why can't it just begin with our need? I mean, God is all knowing, for heaven's sake. He knows what we need before we ask Him, so why does He make us bother?

From what I can tell about Him, I think He usually waits for us to cry out so He can remove all doubt about who came to our rescue. If we never cried out and had no human to credit when the raging fires of our trials turned to embers, we'd likely chalk our deliverance up to circumstantial happenstance or saccharine philosophies like "Things have a way of working out, don't they?"

Things don't just work out. God works them out. Blessed is the one who knows it.

Further, God sees great advantage in awaiting our cry because He is unequivocally driven by relationship. Throughout your ascent out of that pit, never lose sight of the fact that God will forever be more interested in you knowing your Healer than experiencing His healing, and knowing your Deliverer than knowing your deliverance. The King of all creation wants to reveal Himself to you. His Highness is willing to come to us in our lowness. Our cries blow the lid off the cistern we're trapped in. They voice openness. Readiness. That's what God is after.

The kind of cry the psalmist describes can come either from the desperate (I *need* God and God alone) or the deliberate (I *want* God and God alone). Remember, we don't always have to wait until we're desperate. We can wise up enough to know how desperate we're going to be if we don't cry out immediately. With everything you've got, look up and cry out. Open your mouth, say, "God, help me!" and mean it. Bring heaven to a standstill. Get some attention.

Maybe you should do it like a guy I encountered not too long ago. Recently I sat in the middle seat of row six on a packed aircraft, in what I like to call the "getting classier" section, just two rows south of the heavy veil. An attractive thirtysomething couple moved into the bulkhead seat right in front of me with an adorable toddler—and, boy, were they crisp in their Italian couture.

We taxied the runways so long I thought we might as well merge onto the freeway and drive. Finally cleared for departure, we were just beginning that G-force feeling of the pedal-to-the-metal when the dashing young husband began to scream. And I mean *scream*.

I sat straight up in my chair, scrambling to see if he'd been stabbed and we'd been hijacked. His screams turned into bellowing booms I could make out even over the roar of the engine. "I hate flying! I hate it! Ohhhhhh! We're going to crash! Help me! Awwwwh! I hate this! Get me out of here!" On and on for five disturbing minutes.

In retrospect, I wonder if he'd done it before. Not once did his young wife pat his arm and say a soothing word, nor did she ask the more pointed question: "What in heaven's name is wrong with you?" Instead, she glared at him unsympathetically, with a look that said, "Are you almost done?"

Once the pilot turned off the fasten seatbelt sign, the husband wiped off his face, blew his nose, opened his novel, and acted as cheerful as a chimp for the remainder of the trip. The strongest thing he drank was a Diet Coke, but I can't say the same for the threesome right across from him. They never did get the color back in their faces.

When the pilot asked the flight attendants to prepare

the cabin for arrival, all of us in the three rows around Mr. Crybaby braced ourselves for an emotional landing. He was as tranquil as a cat in a patch of sunshine on a nippy day. Go figure.

But wait. Surely he'd be a bit embarrassed when we pulled up to the gate and got up to retrieve our carryons. Nope. He was completely comfortable in his beach-tanned skin. Acted like nothing on earth could be more natural than venting your fears when you have them. I bet he outlives the rest of us. If his wife lets him.

You can cry out like that. Loudly and demonstratively. Or you can do it face down on the ground, making no sound at all except for a groan. However you do it, just do it. And mean it. If your throat is too parched from pain and your soul is too drained of the needed energy, ask God to give you what it takes. Cry out to the one and only God who can deliver you.

After you cry out, *confess*. Think sin, but then think wider. Confession in its widest sense is our means of baring our hearts and souls before God. Confession is a way we agree with what God says about Himself and about us. Confession takes place every time you tell God how much you need Him. Tell Him what's on your mind. What kind of mess you're in. Who's in it with you. What's holding you back. Who's on your case. Who's made you mad. Who's on your nerves. Who's broken your heart. Even if your first impulse is to think it's Him. As long as you can feel it, spill it. Psalm 145:18 says, "The LORD is near to all who call on him, to all who call on him in truth."

All these things are confession, but whatever you do, don't overlook the unparalleled benefit of also confessing sin. Lay it right out there. Let the light of God shine all over your sin so the two of you can sort it out and He can heal you. And while you're at it, don't forget to spit out sins of pride.

Nothing contributes more to the length of our stay in the pit. Pride is the number-one reason why a person who knows better remains reluctant to cry out to God. Confess every sin of your own actions, words, or thoughts that you believe contribute to your defeat. In my own personal journey, God showed me that I'd never break the pit cycle if I didn't name every contribution I made to it and let Him deal with my self-destructive tendencies.

Even if you were thrown into your pit, search your heart to see if bitterness has taken root; if anger, lack of forgiveness, or coldness is building you a home down there under the ground. Examine your heart and see if somewhere amid your loss of control, you sought to regain it with manipulation. Ask yourself if you use your love as a weapon. Get as specific as you can, and when you think you've thought of everything, ask God if there is anything you're overlooking. This process may take days as God reveals things layer by layer. Keep responding when He does.

Not once does God convict us in order to make us feel like wretches. He's out to restore fellowship and to flip the breaker that shut off the power. Remember, God's pursuit is relationship. Confession is one way we talk back after He speaks. He initiates conversation through conviction, and we answer back through confession. Meanwhile, a miracle takes place. Heaven and earth, Immortal and mortal, Perfect and imperfect engage in dialogue. Conviction is a hand-delivered invitation to meet with God, and confession is an RSVP with immediate arrival.

As much as anything else, confession clears the path so the King of glory can come in. In order to get out of that pit and stay out, you and I need the unhindered power of the Holy Spirit. Unconfessed sin clogs the pipeline. If you hold nothing back, neither will God.

The conversation God began through conviction doesn't end with our response of confession. It continues with God telling us through His Word that He forgives us (1 John 1:9; Micah 7:18) and completes in our appropriate and freeing response of grateful acceptance. We will never stay out of that pit until we believe all the way to the marrow of our bones that God has forgiven us. Take a look at King Hezekiah's words to his God in Isaiah 38:17:

> Surely it was for my benefit
> that I suffered such anguish.
> In your love you kept me
> from the pit of destruction;
> you have put all my sins
> behind your back.

Here's how confession works: we lay all our sins at God's feet; He picks them up and throws *all* of them behind His back. In our Christian circles, we constantly talk about putting our past behind us. That's not good enough. It's too easy for us to turn around and pick it up again. We want our past behind God's back. That way we'll have to go through God to get back to it.

The third step out of the pit is *consent*: "Compliance in or approval of what is done or proposed by another . . . agreement as to action or opinion . . . voluntary agreement." Consent is the most beautiful part of the process of getting out of a pit. There is no ambiguity about this step: it is definitely God's will. Determining God's will in so many other areas is less than certain. Like where He wants us to work. Where He wants us to move. Who He wants us to date. This is not one of those areas. God wants you out of that pit. He wants you in victory. Period. So all you have to do is *consent* to what He already wants.

First John 5:14–15 says, "This is the confidence we have in approaching God: that if we ask anything according to his will, he hears us. And if we know that he hears us—whatever we ask—we know that we have what we asked of him." Beloved, God's will is for you to get out of that pit. If you will consent to the process, waiting upon God as He begins shifting, shoving, and rearranging things for your release, you can go ahead and start getting excited, because it *will* happen. Just as God promises in His Word.

When I first introduced the three steps to you, I told you that each of them involved your mouth. I want you to learn to cry out, confess, and consent using God's Word. And to do so, when at all possible, *out loud*. Volume is not the point. All you need is to have your own ears hear it. Why? Listen, beloved, "Faith comes from hearing, and hearing by the word of Christ" (Romans 10:17 NASB). Your faith will be built by hearing your own voice speak the words of Christ.

I have never come up with a more powerful way to pray than using Scripture. One reason Scripture is such a big help in prayer is because our challenges are often so overwhelming that we can't think of the right words to say. Another reason is because we can shift the burden of responsibility to God and His Word. God's Word carries its own supernatural power. It's His very breath on the page that, when you voice it, you release into your circumstances (2 Timothy 3:16).

God loves His Word; therefore, if God's Spirit that lives inside a believer has not been quenched by unconfessed sin, God responds every time He hears it spoken. Yes, faith is absolutely critical to the process, but you can't just sit in that pit until one day, out of the blue, you suddenly have the faith to get out. Let God use your mouth to build up your faith.

Scripture prayers don't have to be used word for word. What's vital is that we echo the principles of Scripture so our confidence can grow in the certainty that we're praying God's will. I encourage you to use your own words, pour out your own heart, and get very specific with God. Don't let up when you begin to feel better. Feeling better is not what we're after. The goal is freedom from the pit *for the rest of your life.*

On days when you feel down, overwhelmed, or discouraged, get to your Scripture prayers all the faster. On the days when you want to do it least, do it most. Be onto the enemy's devices. He knows that if he can make you quit praying, he can make you stay in the pit. When the battle heats up, rest assured that you're worrying your enemy, and he's trying to distract or discredit you. Show the enemy that if he messes with you, you'll just call out God's Word all the more. Nothing does him damage like the Sword of the Spirit.

I'm so proud of you for getting this far into this book. I want so badly for you to be victorious, and I know you can be. God's Word tells me you can. You have the power of the entire Godhead behind you. You have the Father's will, the Son's Word, and the Holy Spirit's way. What more could you need?

And, anyway, what do you have to lose except a pit? So start making some noise. I bet when all is said and done, you end up having a mouth as big as mine.

7

Waiting on God for Deliverance

*G*od can deliver the most hardened criminal or the most hopeless addict in one second flat. With His eyes closed and His hands tied behind His back if He has a mind to. I know people who made themselves at home in a pit a hundred feet deep and a thousand days long—and experienced the instantaneous deliverance of God. One moment they were in the throes of habitual sin; the next moment they were free as birds.

Carolina was one of those one-second wonders. Nicknamed for his South Carolina roots, he's been behind the bars of four American prisons in three different states and is currently serving a life sentence in Louisiana's Angola Prison. Amid thousands of hardcore inmates in what has long been labeled the bloodiest prison in America, Carolina had an inordinate taste for violence that once earned him a reputation as one of Angola's most dangerous prisoners. Get a load of his story.

> Five years ago Carolina signed up for a three-day, in-prison ministry retreat. "I only went for the free-world food," he said. "I was plotting a very violent act and I figured this would be my last free-world food. To me, God was a fairy

tale and anybody who believed in Him was a fairy."

After a day at the retreat, he was bored and getting anxious to leave. He became so agitated that the facilitator started to panic. And then suddenly: "With no preliminaries, no prayer, no blinding lights or trumpets, God just took the violence and bitterness right out of my heart," Carolina said.

"I knew it was gone because I'd lived with it for forty-four years. I thought I'd lost my mind . . . Then I heard Jesus say, 'I love you.' It sounded like words from speakers at a concert.

In every joint of my body I felt Jesus say, 'I love you.' I started crying and I cried for two weeks. I hadn't cried since I was seven years old."

Carolina may still be in a cell, but he's no longer in a pit. Exhilarating, isn't it? Nothing makes me happier than God showing off like that.

I love it. I love to hear it. I love to see it.

But I have not one time experienced it myself. Not one time. Not even an instantaneous deliverance from something comparatively shallow. I won't even be heel deep and still, I'll rarely walk away without a fight.

I'm not a glutton for punishment. Goodness knows I volunteer for instant deliverance the second I realize

I'm wigging. I try to pray and say all the right things, like, "Lord, starting today I never want to think that way about that situation (or person) again. Forgive me and free me of this in Jesus' name. I know You can deliver me. Please do. And, if I may humbly ask, right this second." And next thing you know, all those vain imaginations invade my mind again. They're all I can think about. So God and I have to get back to work.

The process may last a few days, a few weeks, or I may hop from dot to dot in what feels like an eternal etcetera. But I can think of virtually nothing that God has delivered me from overnight. When it comes to high maintenance, I put the "I" in high and the "ten" in maintenance. I've joked with my coworkers that when my life is over, the most fitting epitaph etched into my gravestone would probably be, "God got tired."

Just a few days ago, I was frustrated with myself over an extended family relationship I'm not handling well. I should have more spiritual maturity than to feel some of the things I'm battling. Haunted and hating it, I awakened before sunup that morning and headed out to the back porch where I have my morning prayer time. I didn't even wait for my coffee to drip. I'm not sure I closed the door behind me. I sprawled out prostrate right then and there on the patio.

After I got up off the ground, I resumed a regular prayer time at my porch table and let God reassure me with His love and instruct me with His Word. It wasn't until later that I realized I had specks of gravel stuck on my forehead. I nearly laughed out loud. Some of us, especially yours truly, would be wise to start our day with our foreheads on the floor and live the rest of the day with the floor on our foreheads.

I'm telling you, God and I work hard together. I've come to the elementary conclusion that, to God, *together* is the whole point of any process. Before man was created, God just said something and it happened— "Let there be light" and all. He could still do that. Sometimes still does. But you might notice that a lot of that instantaneous action ceased after man came along, and obviously on God-purpose. Suddenly God wasn't so sudden. God created time for man. In fact, even the words "in the beginning" mark the tick of the first clock. A wait is time oriented and, therefore, primarily man oriented. Perhaps among a host of other reasons, I think God often ordains a wait because He purely enjoys the togetherness of it.

Recently one of our best friends got a staph infection and kissed death on the cheek so many times, we still don't know how he kept from going home with it. His closest friends hovered at the door of ICU for days. We hadn't been together like that in years. Hadn't had time. Suddenly a life-and-death crisis came, and we made time. *Relationship.* That's one of the best things that can come out of a waiting room.

Not long ago, when I battled those confounded

health problems, a loving coworker was a bit mystified over the distraction God had allowed in my life at such a very busy time. "I think He missed me," I told her. In the relatively smooth days preceding the health issue, I had still sought Him and served Him in one capacity or another virtually every day, and, heaven knows, I still loved Him. But smooth living invariably, eventually, makes for sloppy spirituality. I want consuming fire to rage in my soul, and if it has to come through fiery trial, so be it. I want Jesus. A lot of Him. And obviously, He wanted me. *All of me.*

The same is true for you. Maybe we could take it as a compliment. As we discussed in chapter 6, God is driven by relationship. It takes two to tango, even out of a pit. His part is to lift you out. Your part is to hold on for dear life. That's the liberty tango.

Listen, beloved. God does whatever works, whether instantaneous or a long process. Obviously, a process works best for me because, based on our history, God and I really get into it.

You too? Then we're in good company, because apparently God and the psalmist were into a process too. Take a good look at the first three words out of the psalmist's mouth in his testimony of deliverance from the pit.

> I waited patiently for the LORD;
>> he turned to me and heard my cry.

> He lifted me out of the slimy pit,
>> out of the mud and mire.
>> (PSALM 40:1–2)

Obviously instant deliverance didn't happen for the writer of our psalm. He encountered the tick and tock of time between the petition and the fruition. If we approach God humbly for instantaneous deliverance, knowing good and well He can give it, yet He chooses instead to use the wagon of time, He's writing history with each ponderous turn of the wheel, and you're riding shotgun. Good stories don't jump on a page. They toss and turn, ebb and flow, rise and fall, just like the heaving chest of Adam as God first breathed that soul into his brand-new corpse. Life on planet Earth can never be static.

The good news is, we may have to wait for deliverance, but we never have to wait on God Himself. Never have to wait to enjoy His presence or be reassured of His love. If we're willing to take God at His Word, we can have any one of those relational delights instantly. The only wait is on seeing His work manifest in the physical realm, seeing our petition come to fruition.

As you read the psalmist's description of having "waited patiently for the LORD," don't get the idea that he sat around in the mire, sinking deeper every minute, telling God to take all the time He needed. The phrase "waited patiently" is translated from a single Hebrew word *qwh*, (pronounced *kaw-VAW*). Here, the Hebrew *qwh* is translated *expect*. *The Theological Dictionary of the Old Testament* speaks of the "goal-oriented character of the verb *qwh*." The psalmist didn't sit in the pit and twiddle his muddy thumbs until God delivered him. He postured himself in absolute expectation. He had a goal, and his shoulders would not slump till he saw it fulfilled. His Deliverer was coming and, on His way, fighting battles and blazing paths somewhere beyond the psalmist's gaze.

Never fear that God is not at work while you wait. He's doing what no one else can. Get a load of Isaiah 64:4:

> Since the beginning of the world
> > men have not heard nor perceived
> > > by the ear,
> > nor has the eye seen any God
> > > besides You,
> > who acts for the one who waits for
> > > Him.
>
> (NKJV)

If your eyes could only see how God is moving all those chess pieces around the board for maximum impact, it would blow your mind. He's up to something big that affects not only you, but those around you. In fact, Scripture tells us that a thousand generations can reap the benefits of God's gracious favor over one who loved Him and followed Him obediently (Exodus 20:6). God has the capacity to mark your entire family line—be it physical descendants or spiritual descendants you mentored in the faith—with blessing and with the highest privilege of bringing Him glory. He is the One "who is, and who was, and who is to come, the Almighty" (Revelation 1:8). Within every "is," God is mindful of what "was" and what "is to come," and He intends to show Himself mighty in all of the above.

The word *qwh* is also translated "wait" in Psalm 130, where the eager expectation is beautifully clear from the context:

> Out of the depths I cry to you, O LORD;
> O Lord, hear my voice.
> > Let your ears be attentive
> > to my cry for mercy.
> If you, O LORD, kept a record of sins,
> > O lord, who could stand?
> But with you there is forgiveness;
> > therefore you are feared.
> I wait for the LORD, my soul waits,
> > and in his word I put my hope.
> My soul waits for the Lord
> > more than watchmen wait for the
> > morning,
> > more than watchmen wait for the
> > morning.
>
> (vv. 1–6)

The psalmist watched for God like a civil watchman gazing at the horizon from atop the city wall, waiting for the victorious King to come into full view. According to the lexical aids of *The Complete Word Study Old Testament*, the Hebrew word *qwh* means "to lie in wait for someone . . . to expect, await, look for patiently, hope; to be confident, trust; to be enduring." What does a watchman have to do with us? In God-terms, waiting means adopting a watchman's posture. That means ceasing to make ourselves comfortable in that pit another day. Spiritually speaking, stand up and watch. Anticipate your absolute, inevitable deliverance.

As we watch and anticipate, we have the opportunity to practice one other part of the definition of *qwh*, my favorite part. *The Complete Word Study Old Testament* adds to the definition of the word, telling us it also means "to bind together (by twisting)." Let me help you picture what this means.

After a lifetime full of dysfunctional relationships and inevitably unmet expectations, motherhood somehow turned out to be everything I imagined it to be. More than I imagined it to be. Nothing had ever hit me with that kind of gale force. With her almost indiscernible infant breath, Amanda huffed and puffed and blew down the house I'd built around my heart.

Having foreseen and perfectly timed the opportunity, God wisely used my firstborn to make my getting well and becoming a whole person finally worth any amount of work it required. Sadly, I didn't like myself enough to do it just for me. Sadder still, I didn't trust God enough at that time to do it for Him. But He knew that I finally held something in my arms so precious and yet so emotionally vulnerable, I'd do anything not to totally mess her up. I still would.

The stork dropped this surprise package on Keith and me when we'd barely been married ten months. Twenty-two years old and the first in my group of friends to be a mom, I didn't have a clue what to do with a toddler, so I did what came naturally to my sanguine personality: I played with her. Amanda's favorite, hands down, always came at the end of playtime, when I told her that Mommy needed to straighten up the house before Daddy got home. I'd take on a certain dead-giveaway tone, pretending to heap a little guilt, and tell her not to worry—she could go right on playing while I got to work. That was code language for "Climb on." She'd grin and act as if she was going about her business, but when I turned my head, she'd throw her arms around my thigh and put both little feet on one of mine.

Wherever I walked, she rode. I'd start putting dishes in the sink and clothes in the washer, pretending I was oblivious to the tiny tot I was dragging along on my leg. Finally, I'd call her. "Amanda? Where'd you go? I can't find you anywhere! Answer your mother this second!"

She'd giggle her head off.

Dragging her from room to room on my right foot,

I'd look behind the furniture and in the closet, all the while calling her name. When she couldn't bear keeping the secret any more, she'd yell out, "I'm right here, silly Mommy! Look right down here!" I'd glance down with pretend shock, and jump and squeal like she'd scared me half to death. We'd both laugh ourselves silly . . . then we'd do it again the next day.

When Melissa came along, her big sister taught her the game the moment she was barely old enough to stand up and hang on. I'd walk all over the house with those two munchkins atop my aching feet. By the time I was supposed to call out their names, I was out of breath.

That's the picture of *qwh*. While you wait for God to work and to manifest your sure deliverance, you wrap yourself around Him as tightly as you possibly can. Ask Him to make you more God-aware than you have ever been in your life. Bind yourself to Him with everything you've got so that you will ultimately—inevitably—go anywhere He does. Hang on for dear life and never let go. Pin yourself so close to Him you can almost hear Him whisper. His words will live in you and you will live in Him. God does not make His home in a pit. Bound to His holy robe, neither will you.

8

Make Up Your Mind

So how do you know when the wait is over and you're finally out of that pit? Two ways. Psalm 40:2 describes the first one:

> He lifted me out of the slimy pit,
>> out of the mud and mire;
>> he set my feet on a rock
>> and gave me a firm place to stand.

One way you know you're out is when you realize that, after all the slip-sliding you've done, your feet are finally planted on a rock. It means you've found a steady place where you can stand all the way up, resting your whole weight on your feet without fear of eventually discovering you're knee deep in new quicksand. As long as you rest all your weight on that rock, you're not going to fall. Winds may blow and waters rise, but you will not lose ground. Praise His steadfast name, God is not a divine rug someone can pull out from under your feet. He can hold your weight—the full emotional, spiritual, mental, and physical poundage of you—sixty minutes an hour, twenty-four hours a day, seven days a week, 365 days a year for the rest of your life.

I want to emphasize that phrase, *the rest of your life.*

God is not just a firm place to stand. He's a firm place to stay. This book is not about getting out of the pit for a while. It's about getting out of the pit for good. And if that's what we want, we have to do something absolutely crucial. We have to make up our minds. God *gives* us a firm place to stand, but we have to decide we want to take it, and then plant both our feet. That's exactly what the Hebrew word translated "firm" in Psalm 40:2 means. In another psalm, it is used to characterize man's response to God. Psalm 78 speaks of a generation who "would put their trust in God and . . . keep his commands," unlike their forefathers, "a stubborn and rebellious generation, whose hearts were not loyal to God" (vv. 7–8).

That word "loyal" means to be "sure . . . certain . . . ready . . . prepared . . . determined." God's complaint with the Israelites in Psalm 78 was their inability to make up their minds about Him. Were they with Him or not? Did they want a firm place to stand or an emergency room to visit? Like us, they wanted God when they were in trouble, but as soon as the pressure let up, they wanted to be their own boss.

At its very core, loyalty means a made-up mind. It means that certain questions are already answered before life asks them—we don't wait until the heat of the moment to decide. You know what I'm talking about. A loyal spouse doesn't wait until someone flirts with her at work to decide if she's going to be faithful.

She made the decision to stand by her man before a circumstance posed the question.

That's how God is about you. He made up His mind about you before the foundation of the world. Regardless of who has betrayed you and what promises they didn't keep, God is firm in His commitment to you. Circumstances don't cause Him to rethink His position. Even if you, like me, have made multiple trips to the pit, His affection for you is unwavering. He's all yours if you want Him. The Rock is yours for the standing once you've made up your mind that's where you want to be.

I'll tell you why I'm hammering the point. Until you finally make up your mind that you're cleaving to God and calling upon His power from now until Hades freezes over, your feet are set upon a banana peel. You may stand while the wind is calm, but when the storm hits and the floodwaters rise, the undertow will leave you gulping for air. Case in point: my friend with a fierce drug-dependency problem spoke to me recently of her extreme frustration with relapses and her confusion concerning her intermittent bouts of victory. She explained that she does "so well in between" crises. She gets along great as long as her ex-husband doesn't do something to remind her of rejection. She stays consistent as long as her kids don't have problems in school. She pedals along beautifully if she can pay her bills. She thinks that if she could rid herself of the problems that tempt her to drug use, she could stay on her feet.

The problem is, life on planet Earth consists of one crisis after another. Beloved, this I promise you. Circumstances will offer unceasing invitations back to the pit. The fact is, we do have an enemy, and he formulates one scheme after another. He knows how to trip your switch. He finds your Achilles' heel, and that's where he aims his darts. And he's a great shot.

You can insulate yourself from the temptation for only so long. At some point, you have to get out there, plant your two feet upon that rock, and resist. Once, then twice. Ten times, then thirty times, then fifty, till your flesh submits and your enemy gives up on that front. Sooner or later, relying on the power of Christ acting through you, you're going to have to face your foe and win. You can't just run from him and hide, because he'll keep showing up wherever you go.

Something happened recently to remind me of this fact. In our search for a peaceful corner of the West for writing, we intruded on bear country. My tiny writing cabin is nestled in the pine trees and aspens of Teton Forest, where the tranquil beauty can be very deceiving. As long as those aspens have leaves, you have a big threat in a bear suit. We've found paw prints with long claw marks close to the house countless times. We have one preserved on the back of our house where a bear must have braced himself to reach the limb of the nearby tree with his other paw.

Recently we had a change of scenery. Keith wanted

to take a fishing trip on a small sliver of an island in Florida. He took Melissa and me along, promising that I'd be able to write like a dream. What could be more relaxing, right?

Our first sign of trouble should have been the tropical storm we followed onto the island. It left the pond on one side of our rented house swollen with water. Brackish water. Perhaps you can imagine the kinds of things that went through my head when Melissa yelled from the second-story porch, "There's a gator in the pond!" Great. Bears in Wyoming. Gators in Florida. Well, there you have it. Wherever you go, there's a foe.

Welcome to life on our planet. One day we're well. The next day we're sick. At Christmas we get a bonus. In January we're in debt. If your victory depends on the right circumstances, you may as well wave the white flag and surrender to defeat. Just go ahead and take that snort. Gulp that fourth gin and tonic. Binge and purge that pizza. Sleep with that jerk again. Eat, drink, and be miserable.

Or you could make up your mind that you're in with God, standing upon that rock, for the rest of your days. The apostle Paul called it being found in Christ (Philippians 3:9). Whether my health flourishes or fails, that's where I'll be. Richer or poorer, I've made up my mind. In the light of day or dark of night, find me in Christ. Spouse or not. Kids or not. Job or not. I've made up my mind.

When you've made that decision and given your heart, mind, and soul; and when you've given your past, present, and future "to him who is able to keep you from falling" (Jude 1:24); and when you know you're absolutely in, come what may . . . congratulations, sweet thing. You're out of the pit and your feet are on a rock.

Having a firm place to stand doesn't mean life isn't hard and temptations don't come. It doesn't mean you don't sin, although you won't be able to wallow in it like you used to. It just means you've determined your position no matter what comes your way.

With all due respect—and from one who has been there—it's time to make up your mind. Not only for all the reasons we've just discussed, but also for one other. Brace yourself, because it's a whopper. I believe it may well be the biggest challenge of all: that of trying to stay out of the pit while others close to you are still in it.

I don't think I have to tell you that a whole family can take up residency in a deluxe-size pit with personalized compartments. So can a whole set of friends. Yep, right there on 105 South Pit Drive. Looks like a house. Acts like a pit. Make no mistake, a pit is an excellent place for a pileup.

Especially in families. The ties are so close that the same cord that hangs one tangles all. But no matter who is at the bottom of it, no one is a lost cause. No one is too heavy to be pulled out. God delivers with "a mighty hand and an outstretched arm" (Deuteronomy 5:15), one person at a time. Jesus pulls each willing party out of the pit, and with His own scarred hand, by the way, just in case you think He doesn't get our pain.

If you're the first one who escapes a family pileup, you'd think your fellow pit-dwellers would be happy that at least you got out. You'd think your deliverance would give them hopes of their own, but for some reason, that's often not the way it works. Usually, somebody in the family feels betrayed that you felt a change was necessary. They think it means you're saying something is wrong with the rest of them. Sometimes when a person decides to have a mind made up toward God and feet firmly set upon a rock, loyalty to Him is misinterpreted as disloyalty toward family.

Actually, nothing has the potential for greater positive impact in a close-knit group of people than when one decides to break tradition and pursue another level of wholeness. I am convinced that health can be even more contagious than infirmity. Until the breakthrough comes, however, and the Jesus-virus catches, you better glue your feet to that rock. The pressure to resume your old rank can be titanic.

Certainly, no family is perfect, and perhaps none less so than the one that tries to convince us it is. At the Moore home, we've given that up. We're not cynical though, because we know as well as anyone that entire families can be changed. I am currently watching it happen in my own family of origin, but what has already happened in Keith's is nothing less than stunning. He and I have asked God to chase down every member of our extended families and make them His own. To heal any brokenness with His love and make every life matter. We've asked Him for such a mark on our family line that no generation will be without lovers of His Word, teachers of His truth, and followers of His way—right up to the very return of Christ.

If I were a wagering woman, I'd have placed my money on this happening in my family first, but the chase God has placed on Keith's has been relentless. We really never expected to see with our own human eyes much of the change we requested from God in our family lines. We expected to die seeing it in the distance and believing it all the same. Instead, it is happening right under our noses.

Was it worth it? Was it worth being misunderstood? Was it worth being told you think you're better than them? Is it really possible to still treasure what you love most about your family's ways but exercise the prerogative to dump what you don't? You bet it is. Little by little, we watched family resentment turn into at least a hint of respect, and at most a holy jealousy to have for themselves what we had found.

When God performs a dramatic deliverance in our lives, the nature of some of our closest relationships inevitably changes. The healthier we get, the more we realize how unhealthy we were. We find out where we've been motivated by guilt more than God. Or, for crying out loud, more than *love*.

Cooperating with God through painful relationship transitions may be the hardest work of all in our deliverance from the pit. Persevere with Him and trust Him—not just with your life, but also with their lives. You weren't doing them any favors by staying in the pit with them, despite what they say. Keep your feet upon that Rock no matter how plaintively beloved voices call from the pit. Just as you waited upon God for your own deliverance, wait upon Him for theirs. Pray hard for them. Pray Scripture on their behalf. Love them lavishly, but as a Rock-dweller, not a fellow pit-dweller. Your commitment to them from this new position has never been more vital.

Then again, not everybody is family; not every tie of the heartstring is God's will; and not every relationship needs to change. Some of them need to end. Just flat end. I don't know a nice way to say this. Some relationships won't survive your deliverance from the pit. And most of them don't need to. You discover that the pit was all you had in common, and that under different circumstances you wouldn't even have been drawn together. We can hope that this person is not your spouse. If it is, however, start seeking God for a miracle. But if it's not a relationship God blesses, and not one His Word binds you to, it needs candid examination.

Start with the one you're most afraid of losing. Oh,

I know, you think you can't live without that person. But that's not true. You can't live *with* him or her outside the pit. Infused with Christ's all-surpassing power, you are so much tougher than you think you are. God has somewhere astounding to take you, and if you have some people who won't let you go, you need to let them go.

You may ask, "Aren't we supposed to keep loving people no matter how messed up they are?" Absolutely. And sometimes letting go of them is the most loving thing we can do. If the person was unhealthy for you, it's highly likely that you were equally unhealthy for him or her. In no way do I mean to minimize the difficulty of walking away from some destructive relationships, but if all we do is focus on the hardship, we'll never get out of the mud. Our disfigured sympathies will keep us knee deep in the mire, and our love will turn into resentment.

Ask yourself something I've had to ask myself in my pursuit of freedom: Which of your relationships are fueled by genuine affection, and which are fueled by addiction? We can become as emotionally addicted to a relationship as to a substance. Beware of anyone who tries to become indispensable to you. Who becomes the one to whom you repeatedly say, "You're the only person on earth I can possibly trust." If that's really true, then you're not getting out enough. In fact, I'd be willing to bet that he or she is the biggest reason you're not getting out. Boldly identify any "pusher" in your life, anyone who keeps feeding the unhealthy part of you because it feeds the unhealthy part of her. Or of him. Question an inability to be alone. Is it possible that God can't even get to you because of that person? As we near the end of this journey together, I beg you to let no one "love" you to death.

Be brave, beloved. Be brave! Do the hard thing. Let that person go if that's what God is telling you. Exercise goodbye with a confidence only God can give you, and don't beat around the bush when you do it. Has He not commanded you? "Be strong and courageous. Do not be terrified; do not be discouraged, for the LORD your God will be with you wherever you go" (Joshua 1:9).

Say goodbye to that pit once and for all. Living up in the fresh air and sunshine, where your feet are firm upon the Rock and your head is above your enemy's, is not for the fainthearted. It's for those who make up their minds.

9

Singing a New Song

*Y*ou will have a new song in your mouth, a hymn of praise to your God (Psalm 40:3). That's the second way you'll know you've waved goodbye to the pit.

It doesn't matter whether you have a beautiful voice or make mostly noise, you were born for song. And not just any kind of song. Your heart beats to the rhythm of a God-song, and your vocal cords were fashioned to give it volume. That's not to say other kinds of songs aren't wonderful and even medicinal to the soul at times, since music—not to be confused with lyric—is a gift from God to man. It can get to you. Even intoxicate you when you're not one iota the drinking kind.

I found that out for myself a year or so ago. I was invited to speak at a gathering in Washington, DC, and since my firstborn had never been there, I took her along. We were invited to go to the symphony at the prestigious Kennedy Center with once-in-a-lifetime seats in a bird's-eye box. We put on our fanciest duds and mingled with some of Washington's finest as we made our way through the wide corridors to our seats. The whole affair was just like something you'd see in the movies. Something Audrey Hepburn would have attended, dressed just so.

I wish I could tell you that I am an experienced

patron of the arts, but, truthfully, I'm not even an experienced patron of arts and crafts. That night, Ellie May Clampett went to the symphony, and she was sitting in my seat and wearing my hair.

Most of the time I didn't know what song we were on. Nor could I appreciate the guest pianist introduced in the middle of the evening, but I knew he was special. The crowd went absolutely wild. He would play several bars of music, then throw his head back and swing his arm behind him with tremendous drama. You might be impressed to know that I *am* actually a patron of the Houston Livestock Show and Rodeo, and the way the guest pianist played wildly with one hand reminded me of some bull riders I'd seen. I tried to relate as best I could.

As we neared the end of the evening, the songs heightened in a crescendo almost unbearable to the soul. Beethoven came back from the dead, kidnapped my emotions, and held me captive. The last note burst like fireworks, and the conductor's wide-stretched hands hung in the air for what seemed like minutes, as if they'd been caught on the tip of a huge treble clef.

For a few seconds nobody could breathe. Breaking the silence, the woman just in front of me stood up and began yelling at the top of her lungs, "Bravo! Bravo!" I was astounded. I mean, let's face it. We all know what the word means, but how many of us have ever been in a place where they actually used it? This was my maiden voyage into Bravo-ville, and I was bug-eyed. Then, one by one, people throughout the audience stood, and finally, everyone in the great house was on their feet, clapping their hands raw, and I, right there with them, screamed, "Bravo! Bravo!"

Afterward, we made our way into the hallowed halls where every face shone with artistic satisfaction. Indeed, we felt more excellent for having come. As for me, I waltzed out of the Kennedy Center, totally intoxicated by the experience. Throughout our fashionably late-night dinner in DC, I used sophisticated language. I acted as though I knew things I don't. I felt lofty. High.

Close to midnight, Amanda and I fell in the pillowy beds of our beautiful hotel room and silently took in our evening. Suddenly something came over me. It was my old self. I looked at Amanda, and in my characteristically country tone yelled, "What the heck was that?" We laughed until we cried. We rolled back and forth, kicking our legs in the air, sides splitting. Right about then, Cinderella turned back into Ellie May, saddled her horse, and headed back to Texas.

As good as the symphony was, a God-song in the simplest man's soul is more than that. It's not just a moment. It's the unleashed anthem of a freed soul.

Nothing can take a song's place. If its outlet gets clogged, the soul gets heavier and heavier. And nothing on earth clogs the windpipe like the polluted air of a pit.

Beloved, a song of praise to God, even with tears

streaming down our cheeks, is one of the most blatant trademarks of joy in tribulation. You have not let that situation get to you entirely and bury you in a pit until you've lost your God-song. Likewise, you know you're out of that pit when not only have your old songs returned but God has put a brand-new hymn of praise in your mouth.

It doesn't mean we're completely out of the pain that caused our pit or the pain that our pit caused. It doesn't even mean, if ours was a pit of sin, that all the consequences are necessarily behind us. It just means we're no longer stuck. No longer defeated. No longer caked in mud. Our vision is returning. It's a new day. God doesn't hate us after all. The wind is blowing in our faces once again, and once more, hope springs eternal.

I remember vividly every detail in my ascent from the worst pit of my life. I was driving home by myself from church on a winter night ablaze with brilliant stars, still in acute emotional pain from the situation I'd been in. Singing at the top of my lungs with the praise music blaring from my car speakers, I slid back my sunroof and screamed over and over, "I am free!" I was a long way from being out of pain but, make no mistake, I was out of that pit, and I knew—I absolutely *knew*—I was not going back.

What does the psalmist mean in saying we have a new song in our mouths? He means that a whole new level of praise begins to erupt from a delivered soul. It's as if a lid pops off of an undiscovered canyon some-where deep inside, and a dam of living water breaks, rinses, and fills it. A testimony of God's goodness springs from the well to the lips. You have a song on your heart that can't help but find its way—in various words and melodies—to your mouth.

Please pay some extra mind as you read something else that the psalmist testified to his God:

> You are my hiding place;
> > you will protect me from trouble
> > and surround me with songs of
> > > deliverance.
>
> (PSALM 32:7)

If that's true—and God Himself says it is—some of those very songs are playing right now. In fact, according to that scripture, this whole book and every other one like it must be set to music we can't hear. If you've been in a pit, God wants nothing more for you than deliverance, and He has surrounded you with accompaniment on your journey out. Take it seriously. No, take it joyfully. Gloriously! Think of the most dramatic movie you've ever seen. Hear the haunting score of the battle saga *Glory*. The thrilling music of final victory in Tolkien's *The Return of the King*. Hear the football players in *Remember the Titans* singing in the locker room, "Ain't no mountain high enough."

Now, imagine something even better. Surely you don't think earthly movie producers and composers have anything on God. Every Oscar-winning expression of music is a mere echo of the God in whose image the clay-footed composer was created. With all this in mind, can you possibly think that God would deliver you in your real-life drama engaging both heaven and Earth without powerful accompaniment? Without poundings of percussion in the fury? Without weeping violins in the melancholy? Without trumpets of God in the victory? Not on your life. Christ, the King, the Creator of the universe, seeks and surrounds *you* with songs of deliverance.

Can you let that sink into your swollen soul? Can you allow yourself to feel that loved? That sought? That significant? Maybe you and I will get to hear the scores accompanying each of our seasons of deliverance when we get to heaven. Picture God handing us a personalized CD with a victorious scene from the final battle depicted on the front of it. Maybe it portrays the moment a former pit-dweller like me actually won for a change.

But now that I think about it, I hope it won't be just a CD. It needs to be a DVD. We won't just hear the music; we'll see the movie. Only this time, we'll get to see the whole picture: the raging war in the unseen realm that took place over our heads as the angels of light fought the angels of darkness. We'll see exactly where Jesus was and what He was doing while every event unfolded. We'll hear the voice of God commanding the elements to cooperate. Our bonds to disintegrate. And, after all our waiting, we'll get to know the exact moment when God yelled, "Now!" Or at least I think we will. Because our King is a drama King. If He holds the score that contains the songs of our deliverance, why wouldn't He also have the nonfiction movie that the songs were written for? After all, what's a score without a scene?

Until then, go ahead and sing by faith. I know one thing: the music is playing. And who knows? Maybe our souls can hear what our ears can't discern.

If you have guts enough, you might even go ahead, kick up a little dust, and dance. That's what my staff and I did a few days ago. Friday is usually a great day at the ministry, but on this particular Friday, God had outdone the routine. Answered prayers and causes for praise had been rolling in all morning like He was in the mood to show off.

Suddenly I heard music coming from the front office. Music with a beat you could feel in your bones. Then I heard the pounding of stomping feet. "They're dancing!" I said to Nancy. "Let's go join them!" I didn't have to say it twice. She jumped like a jack-in-the-box and nearly beat me down the hall.

While we were in the throes of happy worship, two women walked past the glass front of our reception area, looking for the insurance office next door,

I suppose. They stopped in their tracks and mouthed, "What are y'all doing?"

I opened the door and yelled over the music, "God's been extra good to us this morning delivering a ton of answered prayer. We're just celebrating! Sorry if we disturbed you!"

They laughed nervously, looked at us like we were crazy, and walked on. Undeterred, we danced on.

Seconds later, they were walking through our office door with tears in their eyes. "Do you think you could pray for her?" one asked as she held the hand of the other. "She's really having a tough time."

My staff and I laid hands on that precious, unsuspecting young woman and called heaven down on her and all that concerned her. Christ met Lacey on the dance floor that day to the tune of somebody else's song. That's the way it works sometimes. It's contagious, you see.

> He put a new song in my mouth,
>   a hymn of praise to our God.
>   Many will see and fear
>   and put their trust in the LORD.
>   (PSALM 40:3)

10

Our Pit-Less Future

I dearly love a great ending, and you need to know that we get one. The Author of our faith knows how to finish it. As we wrap up this book on getting out of the pit, I want you to know what happens to the Devil when all is said and done. It's such poetic justice. Revelation 20:1–3 describes it:

> Then I saw an angel coming down from heaven, having the key to the bottomless pit and a great chain in his hand. He laid hold of the dragon, that serpent of old, who is *the* Devil and Satan, and bound him for a thousand years; and he cast him into the bottomless pit, and shut him up, and set a seal on him. (NKJV)

There you have it. Before the Lord does away with Satan once and for all, He's going to give him a taste of the pit. It's the perfect plan, really. And sublimely scriptural. After all, Psalm 7:15–16 promised long ago that

> He who digs a hole and scoops it out
> falls into the pit he has made.
> The trouble he causes recoils on himself;
> his violence comes down on his own head.

After all the dirt the prowling lion has gathered in his paws digging pits for us, he will eventually find himself caged in a pit. Maybe the reason his pit is so deep is because God is scooping it out until it reaches the total depth of all the ones the Devil dug for us. By the time Satan looks at life from a bottomless pit, our feet will forever be firmly set upon a rock. The air will be clear. The fellowship sweet. And the sufferings of this present time won't even be worthy to compare to the glory revealed to us (Romans 8:18). We'll ride raftless in rivers of living water, then bask in the Son.

Until then, life on this battered earth will not be easy, but we never have to make another bed in the bottom of a pit. We'll still have bad days, mind you. But Christ is faithful to stretch out His mighty arm, reach into the depths for what seems the thousandth time, and say in a way we can hear, *Need a hand?*

> He bids me "Rise up," and well He may, for I have long enough been lying among the pots of worldliness. He is risen, I am risen in Him, why then should I cleave unto the dust? . . . But Lord, how can a stone rise, how can a lump of clay come away from the horrible pit? O raise me, draw me. Thy grace can do it. Send forth Thy Holy Spirit to kindle sacred flames of love in my heart, and I will continue

to rise until I leave life and time behind me, and indeed come away.

"Rise up, my love, my fair one, and come away."
(SONG OF SONGS 2:10 KJV)

Notes

Chapter 2: When You're Thrown Into a Pit

Page 21: Spiros Zodhiates, ed.," Lexical Aids to the New Testament," *The Hebrew-Greek Key Word Study Bible: #1923* (Chattanooga, TN: AMG Publishers, 1998), 1,621.

Chapter 4: When You Jump Into a Pit

Page 60: Kurt Richardson, *New American Commentary: James* (Nashville: Broadman and Holman, 1997), 80 (see both text and footnote number 69).

Chapter 6: The Three Steps Out of Your Pit

Page 94: *Merriam-Webster Collegiate Dictionary*, 10th ed., s.v. "consent."

Notes

Chapter 7: Waiting on God for Deliverance

Page 102: Steve Carr,"Set Free in Angola Prison,"
            Decision, June 2006, 8.

Page 106: Spiros Zodhiates, ed.," Lexical Aids to
            the New Testament," *The Hebrew-Greek Key
            Word Study Bible*: #7747 (Chattanooga, TN:
            AMG Publishers, 1998), 1,548.

Page 107: G. Johannes Botterweck, Helmer
            Ringgren, and Heinz-Josef Fabry, eds., *The
            Theological Dictionary of the Old Testament*
            (Grand Rapids, MI: Eerdmans), 568.

Page 109: Spiros Zodhiates and Warren Baker, eds.,
            The Complete Word Study Old Testament,
            #6960 (Chattanooga, TN: AMG Publishers,
            1994), 2360.

Page 109: Zodhiates and Baker, *Complete Word
            Study Old Testament*, 2,360.

Chapter 10: Our Pit-Less Future

Page 141: Charles Spurgeon, *Morning and Evening*,
            Morning, April 25 (Nashville, TN: Thomas
            Nelson, 1994).

About the Author

*B*eth Moore is a teacher and writer of bestselling books and Bible studies whose public speaking engagements carry her all over the United States and the world. *Get Out of That Pit*, the book from which *Delivered* is derived, was first published in 2007, and has sold more than 800,000 copies. A dedicated wife, mother of two, and happy grandmother to two, Moore leads Living Proof Ministries.

Living Proof Ministries

For more of Beth Moore's
ministry and schedule,
visit www.bethmoore.org